SINGLE LIFE

Belinda Barwick's family moved to Canada when she was
three, leaving her with a lasting love of travel and an
enduring loathing of baseball; she was eleven when they
returned to Norfolk. Now a Reader in the Church of
England, she combines a devotion to cooking with a small
kitchen and a devotion to gardening with a tiny balcony.
She loves literature and laughter, and works as a teacher in
a London school.

Acknowledgements

I should like to thank Mabel Brown, Sheila Bruce, Robert Harley, Kitsy Mitchell and Pippa CHN for their help and words of experience when I was thinking through this book.

My thanks to Simon Kingston for his patient advice, to my parents for attending to my creature comforts when I was in the throes of writing and particularly to my sister Hilary for her hours of typing and tidying a scruffy script, as well as for giving me constant support.

Finally I must acknowledge the numerous friends and relatives who may well recognize their *bon mots* here!

MARRIED TO A SINGLE LIFE

Belinda Barwick

I would be married, but I'd have no wife,
I would be married to a single life.

Richard Crashaw (1612–49) 'On Marriage'

TRIANGLE

First published 1997
Triangle
SPCK
Holy Trinity Church
Marylebone Road
London NW1 4DU

ACKNOWLEDGEMENTS

Bible quotations are from the New International Version
© 1973, 1978 and 1984

We would like to take this opportunity to thank those
individuals and organizations who have given us permission to
use and adapt material for this book. Every effort has been made
to trace the owners of copyright material, though in a few cases
this has proved impossible and we apologize to any copyright
holders whose rights may have been unwittingly infringed. We
trust that in the event of any accidental infringement, the owners
of the material will contact us directly.

British Library Cataloguing in Publication Data

A catalogue record for this book is available from
the British Library.

ISBN 0-281-04918-1

Typeset by Pioneer Associates, Perthshire
Printed in Great Britain by
BPC Paperbacks Ltd

Contents

This is for all the single people
Thinking that life has left them dry
Don't give up
Until you drink from the silver cup
You never know until you try.

D. Peek, 'Lonely People' (1975)

Foreword

Some years ago, while serving as a spiritual director at a Roman Catholic seminary, I had the privilege of working with a young man of extraordinary insight. While discerning whether priesthood and celibacy were for him, he shared this with me:

The idea of never marrying has always frightened me, mostly because I don't want to die alone. I was 15 years old when my own father died. He had a heart attack one evening at home, just after dinner. We were living in the country and there was no ambulance and so I had to drive the car to the hospital. He was in the back seat with my mother holding him and he died in her arms. Sad as it was to lose my father, I always felt that this would be a good way to die, in the arms of a spouse who deeply loves you.

Because of this experience, I had never been able to contemplate the possibility of never marrying. Then, one day, while I was praying, the thought struck me that Jesus did not die like my father. He died alone, with no human arms around him. Seen through the eyes of faith, that can also be a good way to die.

Single life can also be a good way to live, though few in Western culture today admit that. This is not surprising since rarely is the single life presented as a state in which one can be a normal, happy person, enjoying all the joys accorded everyone else. We badly need a healthier spirituality for the single life.

This book by Belinda Barwick is not the whole answer, but it is a nice start. What she offers is a map for the road less travelled, the single life. Her map and her tone, however, are not the stuff of the stoic. In her view, the single life need not be a bad situation at all and what she offers is not a series of compensatory notes for those who missed out on first best. No. The view is rather that single life, properly understood and properly lived, carries its own opportunities for meaning and love.

This is a needed book and a prophetic one. It speaks a wisdom no longer in the culture and it speaks it in a way that is devoid of sentimentality and full of the plain practical common sense that is too absent in our contemporary understanding of love, sexuality, family, and community.

Ronald Rolheiser

Introduction

Jesus said, I have come that they may have
life, and have it to the full.[1]

The life of a single person, even in our supposedly
enlightened age, is still often viewed from the outside
as being unhappy, frustrated and ultimately unfulfilled.
'Of course, he never married', people say with a sad
shake of their heads; or, 'She would have made a lovely
wife', implying the waste of a life. Well, for me, life
has never equalled wife, but I do not feel that I have
wasted my time so far! I have certainly experienced
great happiness as frequently (dare I utter such a
heresy?) as my married friends and have both good
memories to look back on and a real hope of an abun-
dant life in the future.

Why has the single life received such a bad press?
Why have single people allowed their image to remain
so tarnished? Why have so many people actually given
in to the accepted view that being single equals failure? Is the single status a 'cross to be borne' or simply
a different way of life? We are certainly in the minority
but do we have reason to see ourselves as a minority
that is in some way handicapped? If we are really to
'give thanks in all circumstances',[2] then surely we
should start from a much more positive attitude,
seeing the single life as a blessing or gift which God
has given to some of us and which should be valued
as such.

1

Being single does not need to be a drawback in life but I am not going to pretend that it does not have its own particular difficulties, just as the married life does. No-one, no matter what their marital status, is really going to be happy ever after, even though that is the romantic lie we have been brought up with. But the myth is that it is those of us who remain single who have really not arrived, not grown up. Look at the terminology: the very word 'spinster' is enough to send a shudder down your spine, conjuring up images of a grey creature in a hand-knitted cardigan with no character of her own, straight out of the pages of a Barbara Pym novel. 'Bachelor', on the other hand, can sound much more desirable ... except that it often seems to be used in conjunction with adjectives like 'crusty old': 'The old bachelor don't die at all – he sort of rots away, like a polly-wog's tail.'[3] What a fate!

The aim of this book is to begin to set the record straight; to help those who are single think through their situation and perhaps to inform our married brothers and sisters of what it is really like on your own. I have not explored the position of single parents or those recovering from a divorce because their experiences are entirely different from my own, but it may be the case that people who find themselves single again may discover their feelings are not dis-similar to mine.

It is very easy to fall into the trap of accepting what others project onto us; to believe, without thinking it through, what we have been told, that single equals sad. We are bombarded with that message constantly, through advertising, through the pages of fiction, through the well-meant sympathy of friends. It takes a great deal of detachment to be able to shake off all those assumptions and to begin to value our marital status.

2

One of the functions of a Christian is to show the world that life is a pearl of great price. It is a pearl that really shows its gloss and sheen when we ourselves become aware of its value. Life – all our lives – are there to be lived and lived abundantly. Do not let anyone, least of all yourself, sell you short on that.

1

True to myself

Each one should test his own actions. Then
he can take pride in himself, without comparing himself to somebody else, for each
one should carry his own load.[1]

It is always a bit of a shock when you suddenly realize
that *you* are the one in charge of your life. Perhaps it is
one of the signs of maturity, that moment when you
become aware that no-one else is going to direct your
life. For me this moment of revelation came when I
had a leaking pipe under the kitchen sink and I finally
accepted that I was going to have to find a plumber.
What a responsibility! How do grown-up people find
plumbers? My usual course of phoning my father and
shouting 'help' would not do, as he was over 100 miles
away. The leak is long since mended but I still find
myself hitting those moments time and time again.
No-one else is going to do it for you. It is your responsibility and you have to get on with it.

Some people get through their lives never accepting that, never taking responsibility, and therefore in
many ways never laying hold on their own lives at all.
And what a lot they miss, just waiting for someone
else to do it for them. While they wait, there are missed
opportunities, situations that could have been entirely
different, and a great backlog of unfinished business
piling up and cluttering their lives.

4

I teach four to five year-old children in a state primary school and it never fails to amaze me that in every class I teach there will be some children who are completely unable to choose an activity for themselves. 'You can choose', I say brightly. 'There are puzzles or Lego or you could do a painting ... what about the home corner ... have you had a look at the new books in the book corner?' They will continue to droop on my shoulder, shaking their head at each suggestion. I produce my trump card – 'How about making something to take home to your mum?' The idea is anathema to them. Eventually, with a rising feeling of irritation (thinly disguised) I say, 'Well, go and make a Duplo model then – off you go.' Thus directed, they trot off happily and produce the model; they enjoy interacting with the other children and are content again. The strange thing is that they seem incapable of making that decision for themselves. Until I take charge (and change the note in my voice – too much niceness is seen as wishy-washy weakness by the average five year-old) they are unable to move on.

This shortage of initiative is sad when you are five. It becomes tragic when you are 25 or 35, or even older. Yet many of us will go on drooping on a metaphorical shoulder unless circumstances force a decision.

The stark truth is that when you are single, you simply cannot have that luxury – if luxury it is. The person I have to depend on is me; the person who will direct me is me and the choices are all mine. But just as the children in my charge could actually be enjoying themselves much sooner if only they could rouse themselves from a trough of inertia, so it can be with adults. Choices are tough but, once made, they can be life-transforming. Being in control is frightening sometimes but it can be a great liberation. I am not thinking of the obvious brave and fearless things like hitching round the Outback, or travelling in a country where you know little of the language, or even going into a crowded pub alone (the latter being one of the many things I still cannot do easily!). Rather, being in control means you can stay for coffee after a church service, not be spoken to by a single solitary soul, have all your attempts at striking up conversation repulsed, and still leave realizing it is their problem and not yours. It means not being crushed when you are told patronizingly, 'We'll have to set you up with someone. Poor Belinda.' (Poor Belinda is seriously considering using her left hook on the offender.) It means holding your head up when a snooty waiter expresses the most exquisite disdain – only with his facial expression; he is much too well bred to express such things verbally – at your request for a table for one. Great Scott, a table for one – do such things exist? Well yes, they do and I would like one please. There is only one of me and no, I am not waiting for anyone else.

In such circumstances I recommend sitting down with great ceremony and having a good internal laugh – it might not do much for anyone else but it certainly restores your own equilibrium.

The point of all these things is that you are not going to let anyone get you down just because you happen to be somewhere alone. As soon as you begin to accept the projected picture – the pathetic social outcast without the gumption to find a few friends of her own – you will become that person. And it is simply not true, not unless you make it true. Most of us, married or single, are alone sometimes. It is when we can be completely ourselves, if we want to play it that way. So why not do that? Why not feel free to be you? Find out what you like doing. Really like, not just go along with because other people enjoy it and want to do it. After years of thinking that I *must* enjoy folk music because so many people I knew loved it, it was marvellous to realize that actually I find folk music depressing and I would much rather listen to Mozart any day.

This is something which single people are really fortunate to be able to do – ask any married couple if they have to compromise about holidays, music, theatre, friends and the answer will almost certainly be yes (unless they have an unusually free relationship). Compromise is simply not necessary when you are on your own. You really can please yourself. There may be those who find this idea selfish but it need not be. It has far more to do with using opportunities and not squandering them.

Self-love . . . is not so vile a sin as self-forgetting.[2]

Making choices for yourself, choosing the best for yourself, can sometimes become confused by an over-zealous interpretation of the Christian ideal of self-sacrifice. Making the choice with your own interests at heart (as long as no-one else is hurt by it) need not be selfishness. An over-simple interpretation of St Ignatius Loyola's prayer, 'To give and not to count the cost',[3] can be downright dangerous, particularly if the cost actually means nobly giving away a gift which God is holding out to you. God calls us to be no-one but ourselves. There is a Hasidic Jewish story of the rabbi Zusya who said, 'At the end I shall be asked, not "Why were you not Moses?" but "Why were you not Zusya?"'[4] It could well be that, far from being noble when we neglect or reject an opportunity, we are actually being rather stupid. God does not ask each of us to tread the same path but to tread our own path, and that will be different in every case.

When I was going through a miserable time a few years ago I was advised to think of myself as someone I was looking after, someone who needed to be shown love and affection, someone who needed reassurance. Seeing yourself at a remove like that is initially quite difficult but, once you have managed to think that way, it can be enormously beneficial. It means that you can think through decisions on a slightly less emotional level, not as someone who ought to be doing so and so, but as someone who is free to choose *a* or *b* according to personal inclination. God can and does speak to us through our personal inclinations. It sounds dangerous, I know, and could be open to misinterpretation as a charter for doing whatever you feel like. But it is always a question worth asking. Am I feeling this way because actually I am a selfish pig (always a strong possibility), or is it because God really wants this for me too?

Each of us has a particular path to discover and those of us who are single are fortunate to be able to follow that path without having the responsibility to consider anyone else. There are less likely to be obstacles in the way, unless of course we put them there ourselves ('I have just bought a field, and I must go and see it . . .'[5]). The important part for us is to be listening in the first place or we will miss what God is trying to tell us. (A friend of mine is wont to question how many bushes the angel had to set alight before Moses actually noticed!) The call, God's call, need not be to anything dramatic – it could be to something which seems exceedingly low key or even humdrum. The distinguishing feature of a true call to anything is that it is a step on the way to becoming more fully ourselves. That must be at the heart of any call from God. Each of us has been made for a specific purpose and with particular gifts and it is incumbent on each of

8

us to discover that purpose and those gifts so that each of us can say, with Isaiah, 'Here am I. Send me.'[6]

All of this might be beginning to sound depressingly sober and serious and worthy but it need not be. (Unless, I suppose, your true self is of a sober, serious and worthy nature. We can only hope and pray that you have a streak of frivolity somewhere in there.) Gifts from God do not just encompass gentleness, sobriety and patience; they also include a lightness of spirit, the ability to laugh and to amuse others, the easy sympathy which helps others to relax, a restful quality, artistic and sporting talents and the ability simply to have fun – all those qualities, in fact, which make us likeable. It is not just nice to be liked; it is often a sign that we have learned to like ourselves. This is of little comfort, I suppose, if you are in the middle of a period of thinking of yourself as a loathsome worm, but nonetheless it is sometimes quite enlightening to stop and think what our good qualities are. (Even loathsome worms have some good features.) For anyone who is very British and modest, it may be difficult to do this without squirming with embarrassment, but it can be helpful, especially if it is done in a prayerful way. 'When my spirit grows faint within me, it is you who know my way.'[7]

Again, the strategy of looking at yourself from the point of view of a benevolent outsider can be constructive. Leave aside all the negative characteristics and concentrate on the positive ones. It might sound introspective and I am not suggesting that you wallow in it – just remember to look for the good in yourself, as you would in someone else.

The strength that comes from this is that we have not depended on anyone else in order to feel good about ourselves. Other people can make a tremendous difference, of course, but in the end the only earthly person you can be sure will be with you throughout your life is you. A lifetime is an awfully long time to be with someone you really cannot stand.

It is just too easy to fall into the trap of filling your life with activities and people and just go on avoiding the basic issue of learning to like yourself. It must be, I suspect, even easier to avoid it if you are married, but if you live alone at any stage of life you cannot duck it. Like many questions in life, it is one that we do not answer once and for all and then tidy away into a neat compartment. As we change, with time and circumstances, the question will come back again and again. Even if the answer to the question is no, I just do not like the person I have become, it is always worth pursuing – God loves us and one or two long-suffering friends have remained faithful, so there must be something good there. Even if it is something tiny, it is a start!

Even when we feel at our most worthless, God goes on valuing us – and he will help us to see what is to be valued, if we ask. He may well also tell us the things we should be ashamed of and the things which we should be altering, but he does not leave us empty and unloved, even if the world does.

For those who are single there is no partner beside us to reassure us that we are loved, and there will be times when family and friends simply cannot help. We have to do it for ourselves. It is not easy but it is possible and in the end there is a particular strength to be found in the whole process.

> It all seemed too good to be true . . . And instead of having an uneasy conscience pricking him and whispering 'Whitewash', he somehow could only feel how jolly it was to be the only idle dog among all these busy citizens.[8]

Ask any harassed parent, tied down with the responsibilities of home and family, what they envy the single person and they will undoubtedly say 'your freedom'. It is also true, of course, that many of us will not be free, with aging parents relying on us or other responsibilities that we cannot escape even if we wished to. Freedom depends on many things and, not least, it depends on money. Without financial independence our lives can be very closely circumscribed. Freedom depends on health, too, both mental and physical. It depends more than anything, though, on attitude. Freedom can be an attitude of mind:

> Stone walls do not a prison make
> Nor iron bars a cage
> Minds innocent and quiet take
> That for a hermitage;
> If I have freedom in my love
> And in my soul am free
> Angels alone, that soar above
> Enjoy such liberty.[9]

Temperament can make a difference to our attitudes, of course, but basically freedom *can* be there for most of us. And very alarming that can be, too. Freedom to make mistakes, freedom to go it alone, freedom to choose . . . . Sometimes it feels much easier to look for reasons not to be free: for every mole who dashes out on a spring morning, throwing aside his whitewash pots and brushes with a cry of 'Hang spring cleaning!', there must be thousands who prefer to trudge along underground avoiding the risks of the River and the Wild Wood. Freedom does mean risk-taking and it means having to take courage. But it can be expressed in small ways at first, if you need to introduce yourself slowly to the idea. It can be expressed in quite ridiculously small ways, when you stop to think about it: it might be something as small as buying a different brand of washing powder, or deciding that you feel strongly enough about conservation issues to join Friends of the Earth, or by voting in a different way at a general election – anything, in fact, that is a sign of our independence. Being married, of course, should not alter any of those examples – we are mercifully long past the age when a woman might depend on her husband's opinion as to which way she should vote – but other decisions are often *not* free for anyone who is married. Having to be considerate should be a part of marriage (although I am sure we all know examples of marriages where that certainly does not seem to be the case), but it does not have to be a constant requirement for anyone on their own. If I decide to stay up until 3.00 am, then I am not putting anyone out. If I want to go on a retreat for a few days, then no-one else is going to have to look after my responsibilities. If I want to go abroad on holiday and *not* decorate the hall, even though it is looking in need of some repair, then that is *my* choice. No-one else needs to be consulted. I am not recommending a regime of self-indulgence but I am suggesting that freedom is there to be enjoyed.

> Take good care of time, how you spend it, for nothing is more precious than time. In one little moment, short as it is, heaven may be won or lost.[10]

Time is a precious commodity – even more so, it seems, in this age than in earlier times. We all say we do not have enough of it ... but I must say that every time I sink down with a cup of tea at the end of a busy working day I feel greatly relieved that there is not a large and hungry family clamouring to be fed. If I want to become a couch-potato for an evening then the only shirts not ironed for the next morning will be mine . . . and years of experience have taught me that it is entirely possible for one person to iron the clothes she will need for the day shortly before she puts them on. Of course I have far more time for all sorts of things than anyone who is trying to run a house, feed a family and hold down a full-time job. But I would add that I do have to run my own home, feed myself and hold down a full-time job.

Sometimes within the church this simple fact is overlooked and single women in particular can be seen as ripe for exploitation. You even hear people say it – 'Mary will do that, she has nothing else to do. She has no family to worry about.' Or, more subtly, the assumption is just made that of course as she has no husband waiting at home, the single woman will be only too pleased to have a little task to occupy those lonely leisure hours. A lot has been said over the past few years about the importance of not pressing the hard-pressed laity even further but the message still needs to be heard. The long-established custom of creating doormats out of the spinsters of the parish is one of the least edifying aspects of the recent history of the Church of England, but single men are not immune in this area either.

What happens can be a sort of conspiracy between those who are not sure how to fill their time and those who want a job done. It is quite easy, when you are single and when you are aware that other people do have someone waiting for them, to assume that you must therefore be the one to volunteer for a task. You can have a feeling of being useful at first (and good- ness knows it is nice to feel that), but later, as the load builds up, the feeling of usefulness diminishes and the resentment of being used grows. It is an enlightened pastor who can see what is happening and step in to counter growing resentment. It is all very sad, especially when it leads to bitterness against the church community.

The only answer is to allow all parties the freedom to say no, without fear of being thought less of for it. It does mean, too, that if you are single you must be able to examine your own motives and to think through whether you really need to go on that committee, take those minutes, organize the coffee rota, serve on the PCC and so on and so forth. It can be quite uncomfortable to discover that our motives were not quite as pure as we had thought and had more to do with massaging our own ego or gaining some sort of power. So, take time to make the decision and do not be pressurized into an instant answer. If it is something that you enjoy doing, or that you would like to do to help out, or if you are wanting to find ways of becoming more involved with the church community, all well and good. But do not enter into a conspiracy which robs you of your time and allows bitterness to develop. It is St Ignatius Loyola's giving and not counting the cost again and it has its price. Married couples can protect each other and each other's spare time – it is an admirable thing to do and shows real concern for the other person. If you do not have someone to do that for you, though, you must do it for yourself. The consequences otherwise can be too destructive.

Your time is not just for church-based activities and being a Christian does not just take place in church. Time is also for friends, family, reading, music, theatre, sports – the things you like doing. Without being in any way selfish about these things, it is important to leave time for them – it is to do with self-identity, self-confidence and most of all, enjoyment.

Here today, up and off somewhere else tomorrow: travel, change, interest, excitement! The whole world before you and a horizon that's always changing.[11]

The opportunity to travel is one of the great pleasures of our times and if you are on your own you can take advantage of that quite easily, once you have convinced yourself that you *can* go it alone!

Holidays can be spent doing rather more exciting things than are possible, for financial or interest reasons, with a family. Most children are not keen to be dragged round an art gallery or a golf club or to trek desert wastes: in fact they often hate to travel any distance at all. My married friends are at their most envious when I go off on holiday, following my own interests! It is entirely possible to travel widely, to explore different countries and new cultures either alone or with a travelling companion. The iniquitous business of single-room supplements must irritate anyone who wishes to travel alone, but it should not put you off trying. Friends who have tried holidaying alone tell me that a week is their limit before loneliness sets in, but if it is something that you feel like doing, then why not? No-one is in charge of your life but you. If you have no dependants then you can take off for the weekend and go somewhere new. Perhaps it would be nice to go with someone but if it is a choice between going alone or not going at all, is there a contest? Getting away for a few days helps you to relax, stimulates your mind and gives you some time when you are not responsible for anything apart from enjoying yourself!

Of course, money can be a deciding factor in how much travelling you can do, and the responsibility of providing for yourself is another major consideration for the single person. It is often assumed that of course you will have plenty and to spare – what can you possibly have to spend it on? Well, living for a start. I don't know whether two can live as cheaply as one, but I do know that getting started on the property market, particularly in such expensive areas as London and the home counties, is not easy. Only having one income does cut down the choices considerably. Having said that, once you have started on the property ladder there is again no doubt that most single people will be less financially constrained than couples with children. It is to do with freedom, but includes the freedom to be pretty hard up and the freedom for things to go wrong. When they do go wrong, a single person has to pull him or herself out of the mire by their own bootstraps. It is nothing to whinge about but it is a fact and when the things that go wrong include redundancy or debilitating illness, the results can be alarming and frightening.

Single people are able to give sacrificially of their money if they so choose. They are able to give of their time and they are able to give freely of their commitment. The chance to commit oneself to a particular mission or cause is not one to be dismissed lightly or to be tossed aside. It is one of the great privileges of the single life. I can make a commitment without having to consult anyone else; I can assume a duty or accept an opportunity and know that the right to that decision belongs to me alone. It does not matter if anyone else thinks that it is crazy – no-one else can deflect me or change my mind, unless I want it changed.

All these freedoms, responsibilities and commitments come back to the one central issue of choice and so ultimately it is worth asking the question, 'Have I chosen to be single?' That is not as simple a question as it sounds, because the answer is not as straightforward as 'Well, no-one has asked me to marry him.' I think it was Germaine Greer who said that anyone *can* have a partner if they want one. I am not denying for a minute that some people will feel the decision as to whether they should marry or not has been taken out of their hands by circumstances. I do suspect though that we are not the powerless tool of circumstance we sometimes imagine ourselves to be. Somewhere inside, at various points, we may have chosen not to take risks, perhaps not to commit ourselves to a particular person. We may have chosen to avoid intimacy. We may have chosen to avoid commitment. We may have chosen not to go out searching for a partner (because that is what the mating game is). If we have decided not to do that, it is possible that the reason for the decision is that we know, taking it on balance, that really we are happily unmarried. We might even regret our decision but nonetheless we made it. By owning the decision and reflecting on the process, we can make our own view of being single rather different. Do you really want to be married? It is an interesting question because sometimes the answer might be 'No, not really. Not enough to give up everything else for.' If I am honest, it would have to be a pretty amazing person who could make me want to give up much of my present lifestyle – and pretty amazing people are not two a penny.

A priest friend of mine who has to advise couples preparing for marriage always asks them if they have explored the alternatives, if marriage is the only option to them. This can meet with a pretty frosty response but it is an important question, because if they are just drifting into a commitment, think what they are giving up!

Even if you are a victim of circumstances, perhaps

for health reasons, or because of a personal tragedy, or because there just are not many potential partners about, it does not mean that you have to give in and act like a victim. Many women of an earlier generation were affected by the huge death toll suffered in the young male population during World War I, but they did great things with their lives and learned, albeit the hard way, that you do not have to marry to be a success.

It is when we accept victim status that we have given in to the assumptions of society and have lost pride in ourselves. Look again at the text with which this chapter opens: 'Each one should test his own actions. Then he can take pride in himself, *without comparing himself to somebody else*, for each one should carry his own load.' We each have our own load to carry and the load varies from person to person. While it might seem unfair that some people do have a loving partner, beautiful children and a comfortable lifestyle, they still may envy us certain aspects of our lives. In the end, comparisons are of no help at all. Life, after all, is not fair – if it were, then millions in the world would not be starving; there would be no innocent victims of crime; we would not be a society of haves and have-nots; and Jesus would not have been killed – the ultimate example of the innocent victim.

Wallowing in feelings of frustration and unfairness is at best unproductive and at worst highly destructive. Periods of self-pity are inevitable in even the best run lives, but do not let yourself stick there.

There is a children's story called *Princess Smartypants*[12] by Babette Cole. Smartypants is my ideal single person and the one whose style I most admire (although her clothes sense is a little way out for my taste). She is very pretty and pretty rich too, and the princes are vying for her hand left, right and centre. She has better things to do with her time, having a magnificent collection of rather hideous pets and does not really want to marry any of the potential suitors. She sets them really difficult tasks so that, one by one, they fail dismally and slink away. Then along comes Prince Swashbuckle, dazzlingly handsome and terribly clever and he manages to complete all the tasks with ease and with a depressingly smarmy grin too. But do not worry: Smartypants wins in the end. She gives him a magic kiss and turns him into a giant warty toad. He drives away (very crossly) in his flashy sports car, so Smartypants can go back to her pet collection and live happily ever after. There's a princess with a bit of sense!

Life is too short to waste it hopefully kissing frogs. It is to be lived to the full and it is there for each one of us, if only we will open our eyes and see.

2

Being alone

But Jesus often withdrew to lonely places.[1]

'I want to be alone', Greta Garbo (we are told) used to cry. 'Why don't they leave me alone?' I wonder if she enjoyed her solitude when she got it? Most of us, married or single, sooner or later, will find ourselves alone and wondering if we like it. There is a fine line between being alone and feeling lonely and, once that line is crossed, misery can set in pretty quickly. While it is true that anyone, whatever their marital status, can feel desperately lonely, it is also true that single people will find themselves alone sooner and certainly more frequently than most others.

Inevitably, all adults have to face up to the reality of being alone. As children we do not often experience it, and the transition from having constant company to experiencing long periods of solitude can take a lifetime, or it may come upon us when we are far too young to find the maturity to cope. It can come very late in life and then can be extremely traumatic, but whenever it comes, it is not easy.

To those in a busy family or community, being alone can appear idyllic. A friend of mine, who is a member of a religious community, speaks of the wonderful, though rare, moments of realizing that she is the only person in the house, while another married friend has been known to bemoan the fact that he has never had a bathroom that is for his own exclusive use! But for single people, being alone is a central issue, one that cannot be ducked, and the way that we deal with it will decide whether we are going to sink or swim.

This does not mean that you have to be tough to survive (although a certain amount of toughness is probably an asset). It does mean working our your own way of dealing with it, but, be warned, it is one of those things that you have never got sewn up, even if you think you have. You may be strolling along one minute thanking God for all the blessings of your life, and the next be knocked flat and railing at him for throwing all this misery your way.

It is unfortunately a fact of life that most of us will not begin to think through some of these things until we are in the middle of a small crisis, or even a large one, and it is not easy then to do a major sorting out of feelings.

The important thing in the bad bits is just to get through – and the experience can be most effective as a learning exercise in retrospect, rather than trying to sort out our personality defects when things are already bad enough! Friends can send out some lethal little bombshells at times like this. From their own secure and settled lives they remark, 'Get out and meet some new people.' ('Just what I'd like to see you do', I'm muttering, 'Go and blight someone else's life with your advice.') How can I find the energy to meet new people when I'm feeling this low?

'You should join a club', or 'Have you thought of evening classes?' are other popular recommendations. The underlying assumption of all of these pieces of well-meant advice is that you need to fill your time and that ideally you need to meet the man/woman of your dreams. (For this reason, women were at one time always advised to join car maintenance classes, on the grounds that they would be full of hunky available men. More usually they were full of women looking for hunky available men.) Actually, of course, what you need to do is to come to terms with being alone and you are not going to do that in an evening class or a club, good though they may be for other reasons.

There will always come the point of having to go home, having to realize that there isn't anyone who is going to be there just for you, and having to learn to use your own resources.

Using your own resources depends on learning to enjoy your own company. This is not just a matter of learning to like yourself – after all, you can like any number of people without wishing to spend 24 hours a day in their company – but actually enjoying being the person you are and learning to enjoy doing things alone; things that are special for you. Having a laugh with yourself may make those around you (if you are in public) think that you are mildly loopy, but on the other hand it can cheer you up no end. It seems infinitely sad to hear people say, 'I don't really laugh on my own.' Try giving yourself permission to do just that. Watch a television comedy, rent a video or read a sure-fire comic novel. The laughter which comes is quite transforming. It reminds us of who we are and lightens the most miserable grey day. It opens that bleak door just a chink so that the Holy Spirit can come flooding back into our lives.

Although events can sometimes overtake us, usually we do make our own luck, we do have control of our own lives and we are the ones to make the choice between wallowing around in angst or finding a positive way forward: 'This day I call heaven and earth as witnesses against you that I have set before you life and death, blessings and curses. Now choose life, so that you . . . may live.'[2] The choice is ours.

What's the good of a home if you are never in it?[3]

One of the things that can be done consciously to improve your quality of life and to build up confidence in the person you are is to make a real effort to make your home your own. We sometimes feel that it is mere selfishness to spend too much time thinking about our own comfort, but married couples do it all the time! It is important to have somewhere, even if it is only a room, that is completely yours. Your home is part of your identity, part of your very being, and can express your personality clearly. Your home is the place where you can have the things that matter to you – books, pictures, photographs, memories. Your home can reflect your enthusiasms and interests as well as your tastes in furnishings and home decor. Of course it should be a place which you can welcome your friends into, but most importantly it should be a place where you feel welcome and comfortable and where you can relax. When you come home dog tired at the end of a busy day you should be able to feel safe and secure and happy with your surroundings. None of this means lavishing vast sums of money, but it does mean spending time. The place where you live will feel like a dormitory if you simply never spend much time there. Never think that it is not worth doing something just for one person. You have as much value as anyone else and, in any case, neglecting your own home does not actually help anyone else.

However pleasant and comfortable your home, though, there are still going to be periods when it seems empty with just you in it. There are certainly times when you will feel vulnerable – there can be a real fear about security and anyone who has ever had a break-in will tell you how difficult it is to get over that feeling of violation and the fear of another attack. There can be a fear of being ill and alone. Having had a very bad bout of 'flu on my own, I would never belittle the horrors of that experience. Looking after yourself when the simple task of getting up to make a cup of tea is completely exhausting is very hard. You feel extremely isolated and lonely. Anyone who is single and suffering from any long-term illness is going to have a very tough time. But people are willing to help when they know of your problems and they will rally round and do the shopping and washing and all the things that you are suddenly unable to do. If you are single you simply have to ask other people for help – and it is worth bearing in mind that most people are only too pleased to be asked.

Some people of course positively love getting in where there is a problem and they can be a nuisance. Parson James Woodforde of Weston Longville in Norfolk wrote this about one of his parishioners in 1798: 'A more officious, busy-bodied Woman in all Cases relating to other People's Concerns I know none. More particularly when ill – a true Jobish Friend.'⁴ Parson Woodforde's frustration with this difficult woman is very easy to understand (and most parishes have one, 200 years on though it may be!), but there are far more genuinely concerned people out there than there are cranky and manipulative ones.

Nevertheless, if you live alone, you do have to learn to live with the fact that you are vulnerable. (A vivid imagination does not help here – some of us are capable of going into the most lurid fantasies of collapsing and not being discovered for days.) This was brought home to me forcibly when a pressure cooker lid clamped shut on my finger. It may have looked amusing, but a lid busily applying 15 pounds of pressure to one finger is no joke. It is also impossible to remove without the assistance of another person. Fortunately my landlady's daughter came to my rescue, but it did make me recognize my isolation. It also made me very careful when drying up pressure cooker lids ever after.

It is the small crises that can make you suddenly aware of how alone you are in your home and how much you need other people. The film *Annie Hall* has one very telling scene where the Woody Allen character has to come to the rescue of his erstwhile girlfriend because her apartment has been invaded by a seriously large spider. You may not need help with spiders, but we all have our Achilles heel!

We all need to have other people around us – 'The Lord God said, "It is not good for the man to be alone".'[5] Unless we are by nature solitary people – and they are rare – it is through interacting with others that we gain our identity and remember who we are. It is through social contact that we are refreshed and any Christian knows that you cannot be part of the body of Christ unless you get out and mix with the rest of the members! So it is important when immersed in work to build in a time to get out and talk to people, even if that is just going out to buy a pint of milk or a newspaper. The most ordinary everyday conversations are important, even when they are on trivial topics, because we just need basic social interaction and without it we can feel very isolated. Anyone who lives alone is physically isolated – it is really disconcerting to get to work and discover that you have lost your voice and did not realize it because you had no occasion to speak to anyone – but it is possible, and perhaps even essential, to avoid mental isolation.

Eating (and cooking) an interesting, satisfying meal does make, I am certain, a great contribution to our feeling of well being.[6]

There are other practical problems to living alone as well as dealing with crises, of course – like the preparation of food. It is annoying to realize that while two probably cannot live as cheaply as one, it takes one just as long to get the average meal ready for oneself as it would for two people. There is always the temptation to wonder if it is worth it and just not bother for yourself. (One of my friends existed for some time on cream crackers and cauliflower – a bizarre combination at the best of times.) But in the end of course it is worth it, because if you do not eat properly you will end up ill, just as your mother always said. I have to confess that I have always been much too interested in eating to fall into that trap! It is worth building up a collection of ideas for quick meals (no, take-aways are not the answer) and using a freezer to store extra portions when you do go to the trouble of making a casserole. If you are in any doubt about how worthwhile it is to go to any trouble just for yourself, do read Delia Smith's *One is Fun*. Living out of tins and just not trying to make food interesting begins to feel like part of a decline in self-image after a while. If you value yourself and your own body then food preparation time is time well spent. It does not have to be Cordon Bleu, just appetising! As Delia Smith says:

> One of the subtlest but, I suspect, most pervasive problems in modern society is that (often carefully hidden) lack of self acceptance, and I really believe that a conscious effort to care for ourselves – especially when eating, which we do two or three times a day – is a marvellous antidote to this.

It is now comparatively simple to buy smaller amounts of all sorts of food – and we are certainly better off than many North American single people from this point of view. When I spent a year in Canada on a teaching exchange I found it verging on the impossible to buy less than a pound of bacon in a supermarket and biscuits came in huge packets. Manufacturers in this country are at last catching on to the fact that an awful lot of people are buying for one, though of course we could wish that some of them were not quite so unscrupulous about making it much more expensive to do so.

Having friends round for a meal is good (not just so that you can buy in larger quantities and therefore more cheaply, though it does give a certain satisfaction) but it is also hard work when you are the person carrying the full responsibility of food preparation, chatting to your guests and making sure that they all have a drink. In an ideal world I would allow plenty of time to prepare food so that it would all be done in advance and I could be charmingly hospitable . . . in practice something always seems to slow me down and I am lucky if I am not still wearing my most disgusting pair of jeans when the first guests arrive (immaculately dressed) on the doorstep. I seem to specialize in kitchen crises immediately before my guests' arrival. If you have never experienced a cloud of moths flying out of the rice container when you rush in to put the rice on to cook, then you are indeed fortunate. Now I know that even married people sometimes have moths in their rice (especially those who buy it from open bins in wholefood establishments – be warned!), but at least they have someone else on hand who can share the panic and then do the potatoes. I suppose that the answer is to keep it simple – or buy the whole lot ready prepared, as another friend of mine does!

It always seems quite unfair that if you want a party for a special birthday or special event, you either have to prevail upon a friend to organize it or do it yourself.

Husbands and wives are forever throwing surprise parties for their spouses, it seems, but if you are living on your own then you are nearly always going to have to organize your own party, like it or not. Downright unjust, isn't it? My answer is to go out for dinner instead, but yours may be different – as long as you remember that birthdays are worth celebrating and that sitting at home pretending it is an ordinary day is not the answer!

> 'Because I want five minutes peace from you lot', said Mrs Large ... and she went off downstairs, where she had three minutes and forty-five seconds of peace before they all came to join her.[7]

In the children's book *Five Minutes Peace*, Mrs Large expends a great deal of time and energy in trying to escape from her lively young elephant family. They even invade her bath – and most mothers will know the feeling. There is no point in her day when she can simply have five minutes to herself. When you live alone, you can have that when you want it and it is a luxury for which we should be really grateful.

Do not underestimate the gift of being alone. It is such a relief sometimes to come in and close the door and know that no-one is going to disturb you. You can even (if you are feeling particularly daring or desperate) unplug the phone as well. No-one can get to you and ask you to do anything. (If you are tutting quietly at my selfishness, do bear in mind that I spend my working day at the beck and call of 30 four year-olds. It can get noisy.) Quiet is wonderful for restoring tranquillity or simply to relax. Of course if your job is not quite so clamorous as mine then you may be less enthusiastic about being quiet, but it might still be worth learning to value something which you have hitherto taken for granted.

In modern society we all tend to rush to fill periods of quiet with sound, to turn on the radio or television or CD player so that we do not stay with the quiet. It is important to leave some space and not just space for prayer. God speaks to us in all sorts of situations and at all sorts of odd times, but it seems to help if he is not having to shout over a stereo, especially if it has been turned on just to fill the empty room. If you are single you have the great advantage of having the time to listen. You do not have to be doing the housework or engaged in good works or even to be consciously praying in order to listen. After all, out of Ignatius Loyola's day-dreaming came a whole new method of prayer. God is not bound by our timetables, even if all too often we are. It is important too to remember to set aside time for God – there is such a temptation to fill up our days and evenings with any number of different activities and then end up with less time than anyone with a family. Jesus was after all a single man – he was not just escaping from the pressures of work when he went up the mountain to pray. He was consciously setting aside time for prayer and we have to do the same. It does not just happen because we live alone – we have to be just as disciplined as anyone else.

> There must be a better way of living than depending on another human being.[8]

When you are alone you need depend on no-one's approbation but your own. Your decisions are for you and your choices are your own. As Christians we are not of course left without guidance – we can all ask for help in prayer and can know that the answer will come to us, but some of us are so programmed to look for the approval of others that we waste hours of our own time trying to please someone else. And what a waste that can be! One of the advantages of living alone is that you soon realize that other people's opinions can be considered but do not need to sway you – we are independent and if others disapprove of what we do, that is their problem.

In order not to slip into arrogant self-centredness it is important to consider our decisions in a prayerful way, bringing them before God. One of the most effective ways of doing this is by regular use of the Ignatian prayer exercise known as the *Examen*. The whole idea of this form of prayer is to develop discernment, so that we can begin to understand our own motives and impulses and to recognize if they are good. It is a useful thing to do at the end of the day, to consider its events with thanksgiving and by asking God to reveal the times when he has felt near to us, or the times when he seemed quite absent! In a time of quiet like that it is possible to discern when we have been operating through selfishness or self-centredness and when our decisions could well have been wrong. God does reveal himself in our feelings and an uncomfortable feeling can be a sign that our motives may not have been the purest! Other people often examine themselves through writing; Tony Benn, one of our more famous contemporary diarists, has said that he uses his daily recordings of events to consider where he has gone wrong. Somehow, putting things on paper – or in his case on tape – helps us to see them with much greater clarity.

I am not quite so brave as the sort of person whom Anthony de Mello describes in his book *Awareness*, the sort of person who genuinely needs no-one and constantly finds the answers in him or herself. When it comes to practical situations I certainly need help and advice; and a friend tells me that for worries about the car he always phones his father and about the kitchen, his mother! But living without depending on another human being means more than that. It means emotional independence, not needing someone else's approval to go ahead with something, and it means not feeling you have to have a partner in order to cope with life. Have you ever known people who reeled away from a very painful divorce or separation and instantly started looking for a replacement? Why on earth does anyone do that? It must be because they feel that they are simply not viable as a single unit. But for most people it must surely be true that a period of living and functioning alone can be valuable and a really important way of finding strength.

Our culture and society are so imbued with the concept of having to be part of a couple in order to function at all that it is easy to be swept along on that wave. Someone – a stranger – recently told me that I was not coping with being single. 'Oh yes I am', I said. 'No, you can't be', was the reply – 'and if we could see your future then you will not cope.' Yes, staggeringly rude, isn't it? I replied that as I had coped for the last 40 years or so I did not expect a sudden decline. (Keeping my cool admirably, I thought.) The riposte brought in a new line – 'You must be after other women's husbands then.' No I'm not; yes you are; no I'm not .... Now, while this conversation broke new ground in terms of downright cheek, the underlying assumption was nothing new: no-one can cope on their own without nursing a hidden misery and if you are coping it is because you are up to no good. Neither of these things needs to be true but all sorts of people believe them, sometimes including the people who do cope alone. If you are living alone then just stop and think: do you sometimes feel bad about it purely and simply because other people expect you to? You really do not need to accept anyone else's projected expectations or sympathy. To live with the knowledge that you function very well on your own can only do your self-image good. Never mind what other people say.

This is not quite the same as 'I care for nobody, not I, if no-one cares for me',[9] but it does not do you any harm at all sometimes to get your chin up and think I *can* do it, I *don't* need to rely on another person. This is Anthony de Mello again: 'You can become happy not being loved, not being desired or attracted to someone. You become happy by contact with reality.'[10]

If you can be honest with yourself about your feelings and emotions and if you can begin to analyse why you feel lonely, then you may well find that it is because you are accepting the view that you should feel lonely. You do not have to accept anyone else's view of your life.

Of course we are influenced by the opinions of those around us, but there is no reason why a single person should feel that they must be miserable or incomplete or any of those other strange things that people think. Being honest and being in contact with reality is a much more sound way of living your life.

> She says, 'Are you married?' (She asks him every time, never remembers.) He said, 'No Mrs Whittaker. I am married to God.' She says, 'Where does that leave you with the housework?'[11]

Being single, as Mrs Whittaker in Alan Bennett's monologue indicates, does leave you with the housework to do. All the rather tedious necessities of housekeeping – the shopping, cleaning, washing, decorating – come back to one person. Annoyingly, it is often assumed that the time you will need to spend on these domestic pursuits is minimal because, after all, you 'only have yourself to worry about'. In practice, it is often the case that a single person will have nearly as much to do as any couple and will have to do it alone. No-one else will feel obliged to come in and do it for you. (Mothers sometimes seem to be struck by an overwhelming urge to roll up their sleeves and do the spring cleaning as soon as they enter their off-spring's home but my own mother has never been prey to such compulsions.) No-one should be so busily engaged on the humdrum routine tasks that they miss out on something really exciting, but in the end we are responsible for the cleanliness and smooth running of our own homes, for getting the decorating done, cutting the grass, watering the plants – the list can go on and on. It may be for our own comfort that we are doing all of these things but they hardly come into the self-indulgent category. Churches can some-times exert a subtle pressure on the single person to give up their time, but who benefits if we live in a perpetual mess because we are never left with enough time to get the hoover out? We were told to love our neighbours as ourselves rather than to fail to look after ourselves at all.

Unless we have the personality type that does not notice dirt and disorder, living in a tip has a demoral-izing effect. When I had the 'flu badly and was unable to do so much as lift a duster for several weeks I reached the point in my ill and enfeebled state of thinking I could not possibly let anyone over the threshold for fear of shocking them with a glimpse of such squalor. (I always over-dramatize things when I'm ill.) When we do look after our own homes and make them a pleasant place for us to be in we are undoubtedly adding to our own feeling of wellbeing and that can only be good.

Alone, alone, all, all alone . . . .[12]

There comes a point in every single person's life – in fact in everyone's life, I suppose – at which we have to face the loneliness that has been lurking around our consciousness for months or even years. Hiding from it and filling the time and putting on loud music and busying ourselves eventually has to stop – and then what? Have you ever found yourself staring into the mirror and thinking, 'Who is that?' Don't do it for long, because it is a sure road to a breakdown. Quite literally facing yourself in the mirror, seeing yourself as a stranger, raises so many questions that you simply cannot answer them on your own. So rule number one is: do not look in the mirror too long, either literally or figuratively. Staring at yourself and analysing yourself and your feelings is interesting as a short-term occupation but too much introspection addles your brain. If you really need help, see a therapist – don't try a do-it-yourself regime!

But the loneliness – what do you do about that? Well, to start with, do not believe those pious platitudes about never being alone if you are a Christian – you are and you will be, and there will be times when everyone, even God, even Jesus, seems very, very far away. Everyone has deserted you and fled and you are just not in a fit state to go looking for them. That is undoubtedly when it is hardest to hold on, when life feels like being adrift on some awful, empty sea. I can remember when I first lived in a flat on my own, feeling, almost tangibly, a chasm right in front of me. As I opened the front door it was like a pit that I had to edge around, clinging to the walls. And once past it there was little consolation – just an empty set of rooms, when I craved company. Now I know that I could have made the effort, could have phoned someone and got out of there – but I suspected then and am sure now, that it was something I had to do. You can only put off the showdown for so long – sooner or later it has to come.

Of course that feeling can return at any time. I have a strong antipathy to snow, because I know that snow equals loneliness for me – everyone stays at home, locked up in their cosy partnerships and the roads are too treacherous for much travel in pursuit of company. But nothing can ever be as bad as that first nightmare encounter with loneliness, because the next time you will know that there is another side to it, that there will be light at the end of the tunnel. You do not know at those times of complete dereliction that you are being held but you are, and what seems like a bottomless pit is really full of the love of God, buoying you up and keeping you afloat. But make no mistake about it, it hurts, and it is something which you have to get through in your own way and in your own time. Other people can help but they cannot fish you out of it, and they cannot do it for you.

Married or single, that loneliness is at the heart of human existence, so perhaps those of us who are on our own are in with the advantage of having to face it early on. There is no-one else to fall back on, there is no other person in whom all our trust is placed – it has to be placed in God, for only he gives us real hope. That self-reliance which we all have to acquire in Christian terms means learning to rely on God. That is not a pious wish, it is a firm reality.

We have a God who knows what it is to be one human person alone, because that is what he was in the person of Christ. When God became human he took on all those feelings and emotions – and experienced that utter desolation for himself. In Glasgow's Mungo Museum there is a famous painting by Salvador Dali, called 'The Christ of St John of the Cross'. The crucifix is at an angle pointing downwards and the world is represented by a lake and a few tiny human figures at the bottom. The absolute isolation of the figure on the cross is almost too much to bear, but it *is* bearable because beaming down on it, and throwing a strong shadow across it, is the light of God shining down via the cross to bring light to the world. God himself knows what it is like to be you or me, and however lonely and isolated we may feel he is there with us, shedding his light in our darkness.

But meanwhile of course we simply have to survive – so what are the survival mechanisms to get through the difficult times? One of the useful things to do is to try to recognize patterns, so that you will be ready to cope with a bad patch. I always find January and February difficult because I frequently go down with a minor illness at that time (the penalty of working in close proximity to 30 human germ-banks) and because the weather is dull and the days are short – a grim time of year. So I can at least recognize that things could be difficult and make plans accordingly. Some friends tell me that New Year's Eve is a bad time – 'Another year gone, what have I done with the old one? What have I done with my life . . . ?' Again, if you know it is going to be difficult and think you will probably be alone, then why not have a self-indulgent evening when you read a favourite book, make or buy yourself your favourite foods and eat the best chocolate ice cream you can lay your hands on? (I recommend Häagen Dazs Belgian chocolate.) Why not have the odd glass of wine or spirits? You are not going to become an alcoholic overnight because you have the occasional drink alone. If there is no-one else to provide you with a treat, don't feel guilty about getting one for yourself. This is all a long way from gorging so much that you become obesely fat, or relying on alcohol to such an extent that you have a real problem.

There are dangers in any self-indulgence but an occasional treat is not the first step on the slippery slope unless you are uncommonly susceptible.

There are lots of survival mechanisms for the low times which are there to be used – telephone, television, radio, books – and what does it matter if it is escapism? Sometimes we all need to escape. The important part is to recognize when we are escaping rather than kidding ourselves that it is real life. But if real life gets too much for one evening then why not? It is better than popping pills.

In the longer term there are other things that can be a terrific consolation – many people find pets a real lifeline. Something to talk to and to look after – something that relies on you for its existence. We all need to feel needed. Looking after plants both indoors and out can provide an important outlet too; even if you are not a gardener it is good to be reminded that other things need caring for apart from yourself. If you are a gardener you will know already how calming and therapeutic it can be to get your hands in the soil, to get in touch with growing things and the patterns of the seasons. It is the best stress-controller that I know of and the reward for your efforts will be immensely enjoyable, even if it is just one brightly flowering windowbox.

> Alone you stood before God when he called you; alone you had to answer that call; alone you had to struggle and pray; and alone you will die and give an account to God. You cannot escape from yourself, for God has singled you out.[13]

Any alien landing from outer space and using our media as a guide might be forgiven for thinking that the be all and end all of human existence is to get into a couple as quickly as possible. Anthony Giddens,

Professor of Sociology at King's College, Cambridge, says, 'To be in a couple is now more important than being married if one wants to avoid loneliness and social disapproval.'[14] But as he goes on to point out, coupledom 'by its very nature . . . is enveloping, threatening the very individualism which it also presumes.' Christians have to stand up to that sort of pressure; we have to resist it and we have to point to another way. Every individual person is important and has value, whatever their marital status and whether they live in partnership with someone else or not. If we deny that then we are denigrating the lives of a growing minority within our society and a large number within our churches.

Single people themselves can be just as guilty of this as anyone else, accepting that their lives are not as complete as other people's. But it is entirely possible to live a rounded life and to live it alone. If we fail to value the single life when we are single, then why should anyone else value it? To be constantly pining for something we do not have is both unproductive and demoralizing, not to mention time-wasting. Inevitably some people will find themselves single because of a tragic love affair or an unrequited passion, but there are few romantic encounters, however sad in outcome, that need be permanently scarring. I am not denying the deep hurt that can linger on for many years, but in Christ the deepest hurt can be healed. This might sound glib and those of us who have had our hearts broken would not have agreed at the time, but it is true and must be true for our own mental health. A life spent looking back, being a sort of latter-day Miss Havisham[15] is not a Christian life.

> Like one that on a lonesome road
> Doth walk in fear and dread,

And having once turned round walks on,
And turns no more his head;
Because he knows, a frightful fiend
Doth close behind him tread.[16]

The spectre of loneliness is always just behind anyone who lives alone. But, like Lot's wife, we soon learn
that looking back at it is not usually a good idea, and
unlike Lot's wife we always have second chances and
third ones. Of course loneliness is painful, it is ghastly
when you are in the midst of it. God does not leave
any of us stuck there for ever though and there is
always a way forward. Even the worst times will pass
eventually and, small consolation though it might be
at the time, you will be all the stronger for the
experience.

3

Friends and relatives

A friend loves at all times and a brother is
born for adversity.[1]

I was once leading a discussion in a church on the
subject of the single life, when I was completely
floored by one comment. It came towards the end of
the evening and the speaker said, with an air of one
imparting comfort, 'Never mind, Belinda, at least you
won't have anyone to mourn.' While this remark does
register on the extreme end of the insensitivity scale,
it expresses something which many people assume to
be true: that is, because a single person has no emotional commitment to one other person, she or he has
no emotional commitments, full stop. My own experience is that quite the reverse is true – because I am not
committed to any one person, there are a large number of people who matter rather a lot. Relationships
with family and friends alike are vitally important.
Emotional commitment need not be the sole preserve
of romantic love: it is to do with family ties, with interests held in common, with lives that have intertwined
for all sorts of reasons.

Many people will assume, albeit with the unthink-
ing superficial part of their minds, that only those
involved with romantic love will understand what love
really is. We as Christians know better: St Paul's
famous description of love[2] in fact has nothing to do

with romantic love, even though it is frequently read at wedding services. It is about the love of God, lived out by Jesus and in the lives of his followers. It is about the steadfast and selfless love which Jesus showed: 'As I have loved you, so you must love one another.'[3] 'Greater love has no-one than this, that one lay down his life for his friends. You are my friends if you do what I command.'[4] What higher ideal of friendship could you find than that?

The family offers us the first step beyond self-love.[5]

It is always irritating to hear your situation spoken of as one who 'has no family' or 'no family to worry about', implying that life is therefore a piece of cake. Most of us do have families and responsibilities towards them. For many unmarried women in particular the burden of caring for elderly or infirm parents or siblings has fallen to them, and a very heavy and isolating burden it can be. Of course what is meant is that there are no children involved and that single people have only themselves to think about and the usual conclusion is that they will probably have become selfish. Of course it is not true, but it is a widely held generalization. When couples choose to marry later in life there will always be someone to say, 'He's become selfish and set in his ways – there'll be trouble there!' Most people, married or single, can become set in their ways, and single people do not have the monopoly on selfishness.

It is not selfishness to enjoy what we have been given, or to use opportunities. It is not selfishness to have become used to a particular pattern of doing things or an established routine. It is not selfishness to spend the money we have earned on things for ourselves. Selfishness only comes into the picture when we lose our awareness of other people or have no ability to empathize with the feelings of others. Selfishness arises when we put ourselves at the centre of our attention and forget about God. There is always hope for a change, even then. Think of Zacchaeus. We are not told that he was single, but he had obviously lived a self-centred life and considered no-one else in his desire to claw as much money as he could into his coffers. Yet after that encounter with Jesus he could not remain selfish. Instead he repented instantly, faced up to his faults and decided to change. No-one has to stay selfish.

As children, we were all at one time completely self-centred. Some of the four year olds whom I teach have a real problem in understanding anyone else and cannot see things from another's point of view. They are genuinely puzzled when asked to think of other people. 'Why?' they ask in bewilderment. 'Don't you know that I'm very, very important?' their expression implies. With maturity this egocentricity fades and most people become more considerate and more able to see themselves as one of a group rather than as the star at the centre of their known universe. It is our families of course who help us do this at first, but as time goes on it will be our classmates, neighbours and friends as well. We move towards a more considerate way of operating. We learn to share and to care for others. For this reason most single people will need their families quite badly: we need to be reminded that there are other people who matter. Lessons like that need constant reinforcing.

We need our families as well to give us a sense of belonging, and a sense of identity. There is something rather comforting about a family resemblance, as if the likeness to a parent or cousin or sibling helps to underline who we are. Our families help to define us – there are the family jokes, the special language, the established routines, the family history and the shared memories. With our families there is a closeness of understanding, all those things that can remain unspoken. Which is not to say that all families operate in an atmosphere of sweetness and light. They can be extremely stressful and full of discord. But unless the family is actually dysfunctional, each member of it will have a particular role and will continue exercising it for many years.

That role need not necessarily be a particularly laudable one; in going back to the family home we may find ourselves reverting to childhood, squabbling like eight year-olds or ordering others around in the most extraordinary way. It can be disconcerting, realizing that you really have not improved or grown up at all, that you are still undeniably you. You may have moved on and you may certainly wish that certain things could be forgotten. (Cute as you undeniably were as a two year-old, do these things need to be resurrected at every single family gathering?) But you cannot – or should not, if you want to preserve a sense of who you are – deny your family's influence.

Those of us who have not done the expected thing and moved on to create the next generation, to pass on the family traditions and history, may certainly feel the pressure to do so. My niece recently told me severely that she should have two uncles, if only I had done the right thing and acquired one for her. Thank heavens her other aunt had a more adequate grasp of her responsibilities. (That is without going into the whole matter of being thwarted in her ambition to be a bridesmaid.)

It is in the nature of a family to want to continue the family line. Such a unique thing should not be lost, we feel. We are too special not to go on. In truth, many of the unmarried family members will be the very people

43

to hold family traditions together. They will not be influenced by duties to another family and generations of maiden aunts and bachelor uncles have given time, stability and a listening ear to the younger generation. An adult who is not in the parental role with all the baggage that goes with it can be of great importance. (Godparents are useful for this role too, so do not despair if you have no nieces or nephews of your own!) Anyone's role or influence within the family is directly related to how much time, effort and commitment is put into the relationship. It is entirely possible for a single person to be one of the key family members, the person who is looked to as the arbitrator, or who sets a particular stamp on the family. You do not have to be a biological parent to carry out that role. It is a decision and not always an unconscious one, that you will spend time on that relationship. While not regarding myself as a model aunt, I do expend some energy on that part; I have tried to establish traditions for my sister's children: a summer outing, the Christmas drive to Granny and Grandad's house, birthday treats – it is not spectacular or expensive or original but I suspect that it is the stuff of memories, and one of the greatest gifts you can give to a child is a happy memory.

For any family to function well, there has to be a degree of trust as well as familiarity, a sense of love at its centre as well as mere intimacy. For any single person it is a two-way process – you have to put the love in to get any back. No-one is obliged to love their uncles or aunts just by reason of the relationship. Actually no-one is obliged to love their parents either, but that is a better-kept secret. Love is not to be confused with sentiment or duty, even though most families are capable of sentimentality and some certainly major on the duty aspect. Love, if we are to use God's love as our model, is given unconditionally, is strong and reliable and never failing.'It always protects, always trusts, always hopes, always perseveres.'[6] It is not easy to love your family in that way, expecting nothing in return, but it is worth striving for.

> Those who know Bertram Wooster best are aware that in his journey through life he is impeded and generally snootered by about as scaly a platoon of aunts as was ever assembled.[7]

I would not wish to give the impression that all families are good and yours can be too if only you would try a bit harder. Difficulties and differences of opinion arise in the best and most loving of families, and inappropriate assumptions can be made and left unchallenged. Families can be very difficult indeed, a place where duty comes before love and where shared characteristics are downright worrying. (Are you really going to turn out as bad as the rest of them?) They can certainly be places where sacrifices are expected and where to question the authority of one or two key members can bring down the wrath of a powerful group upon you. If this is the case, then the single person has to make his or her mind up between facing the fray, putting up with it, or getting out fast. I say the single person because we will generally be the ones with the freedom to choose. We will not be bound by the same ties which hold those who are married or are parents, although our decision may well alter the future of the whole family. Standing up to a dictatorial parent, questioning the way that things have always been done or simply refusing to conform can be the catalyst for change, whether for good or bad. We can be extremely powerful, if we choose to operate that power.

Some families can create demands which are entirely unreasonable, where one family member is assumed to be the unpaid, unrecognized child minder or the doer of all the difficult jobs. It is easy to accept the projected guilt for not getting married and having children and to be forced by that guilt to accept your fate. The pages of fiction are bristling with the put-upon unmarried child. None of us, though, need accept the role of Cinderella and a role cannot be projected onto anyone who simply refuses to accept it. Certain things need to be done but, as Martha was shown, you do not have to be rushing around feeling virtuous to be doing the right thing.

In some cases family members will presume on the relationship to interfere or dictate certain duties. Only think of poor old Bertie Wooster and all the terrible tasks which his aunts impose upon him. A fearsome group of women, ludicrously overdrawn, but exerting power in a way that is not uncommon. Forceful personalities can bulldoze all sorts of people into doing their will, as blatantly as Bertie Wooster's aunts or, more subtly, by charming others into submission. Perhaps we all do it to some extent, but no-one should feel obliged to give in to that pressure, and perhaps it is quite a good thing for the bully to be refused sometimes!

Your people will be my people and your God my God.[8]

One of the most perfect pictures of family devotion in the Bible must be the story of Naomi and Ruth. Bereaved and left on their own, the two women find great strength in each other and eventually find true happiness. Ruth has left her own people and her own country to go back with her mother-in-law to Bethlehem; she spares no effort to support her, so much so that word of her devotion has gone before her.[9] At no point does either of the women try to direct the other – in fact, Naomi does her best to encourage Ruth to leave her. There is no manipulation, no pulling of rank, there is simply love. Ruth's love is better than seven sons, we are told – no family, in other words, could be more blessed. This love does not come purely from the marriage connection but from simple family affection – and that, at its best, is something for which nearly all of us are able to strive.

St Paul is quite clear that we all have a responsibility to our families. In his first letter to Timothy he says, 'If anyone does not provide for his relatives, and especially for his immediate family, he has denied the faith and is worse than an unbeliever.'[10] To balance that we have Jesus' question, 'Who is my mother, and who are my brothers?'[11] He pulls us away from looking inwards, towards a narrow interpretation of family values, and points us instead to a wider sense of 'family'. It is our individual responsibility to work out how much time and commitment we put into family relationships and to ask ourselves whether we are using our families as an excuse for not doing something! Sometimes our supposed filial devotion may be no more than a cover for avoiding something far more challenging, be it a new job or a chance to work abroad.

It all comes back to refusing to accept anything – least of all ourselves and our actions – unquestioningly. We are all capable of some pretty subtle avoidance, masking it all the time with tags of 'duty' or 'sacrifice'. While not wishing in any way to denigrate the work of those who care for the sick or elderly relatives, it is important for all of us to remain realistic about our motives. It may suit a single person sometimes to have created a situation where someone else depends on them: I do not have a husband or wife to devote myself to, so I'll just have to be kind to Auntie Mavis. The desire to be useful can actually be very trying for our families, especially when it is a cover for not growing up and facing our own particular responsibilities.

Terry Jones and Michael Palin invented a wonderfully dull family member in the person of Eric Olthwaite in their *Ripping Yarns* series, screened in the late 1970s.[12] Here he describes their difficult family relationships in his own irrepressibly boring style:

> 'As soon as I raised an interesting topic . . . me mum would always find something else to do . . . or she'd be too busy . . . Sometimes she'd feign death just to avoid talking to me. It was the same with me dad . . . He'd pretend to be French when he came in, hoping I wouldn't talk to him.'

Eventually the whole family have had enough and do a moonlight flit, leaving poor old Eric to be boring on his own. Every single person has to declare independence from their family sooner or later, preferably before the family gets to breaking point!

Parents will often assume that their children have not grown up if there has not been a wedding ceremony to mark the fact formally. They can become dependent on their single children, as a way of keeping control, or indeed single children can remain over-dependent on their parents. This sort of dependency can restrict the lives of all concerned. If we are to be fully rounded adults we must recognize and value our own independence.

> True friendship, like marriage, calls for loyalty. It involves sharing at many levels. It too is a means of grace for the growth of our personalities. It can greatly enhance the quality of our work or of our general service to others.[13]

The well-known aphorism that 'everyone needs friends' is true of no-one more than the single person.

If you are single, you need people you can rely on, people who are just on the end of a phone, people who really do not mind when you have the most self-indulgent whinge to get all your worries off your chest. Do not overdo it though; the average whinger loses more friends than you would believe possible. If you are relying on the telephone to get you through every evening, it is time to stop and consider the effect you may be having on your long-suffering friends.

One of the difficulties of our friendships is that they nearly always require effort and there are certainly times when you just do not have the energy to make the effort. It would be lovely sometimes to have someone with whom to watch mindless television (well, not too mindless – something Inspector Morse-like, perhaps), but I rarely find myself in the position of phoning a friend to say, 'Come round and collapse in front of my telly rather than your own' – it all entails putting myself (and them) out a bit. One of the things I envy my married friends more than anything else is having someone right there to relax with – no forward-planning necessary.

For all of us, friendships need to be worked at; they cannot be assumed to be there unless there is a real effort on both sides to keep them going. It means a commitment of time and that is not always easy when lives are busy. With some friends now I have found that the only way to ensure that we see each other regularly is to put another date in the diary straight-away. If we can simplify the process it takes away the possibility of stress. It is ridiculous (but not unheard of, in my life at least) to find yourself feeling stressed about a meeting with a friend, wondering if you can fit them into your busy life. Crazy! These are the people you should be relaxing with. But for any single person the onus is on us to act – we cannot stay at home and expect the world to beat a path to our door. It is difficult to maintain the effort sometimes, if you are feeling tired or under the weather or depressed, but the alternative is being alone, which is not likely to ease any of those conditions.

> If we are fortunate enough to be in a position in which many people ask for our attention, we must choose those among them whom we are actually to love.[14]

It is important to bear in mind that some people will be more demanding than others, by reason of temperament, or need, or a downright manipulative character. You have to guard against being pulled too many ways, and in some cases that means getting quite tough with yourself and setting some strict parameters. It means making clear to some people that you cannot see them weekly or speak to them on the phone nightly because, if you do, no-one else will get a look in. Being tough also means that you leave time for yourself (I've been putting a weekly 'me' night in my diary for years now – yet another survival mechanism!). It means being aware that some people will use any means, fair or foul, to control those they call 'friends'. You will feel the most arrogant, unloving person in creation sometimes, but you just have to put your foot down and refuse to be manipulated. Beware of emotional blackmail, subtle hints of duty, the application of the 'I knew I could rely on you' technique. You do not need friends like that. A sense of duty, or of being beholden, simply kills a friendship. We may be commanded to love one another but there is no requirement to be a doormat. Doormat friendships do not do much for either side – and for the subservient half it will just lead to resentment and bitterness. Of course we should be accessible to our friends, but giving too much can be harmful; and when there is no spouse to put his or her foot down, we have to do it for ourselves. It requires self-discipline, and you have to remind yourself that you are not being a heartless cad!

It is worth stopping to consider where the whole issue of need comes into friendships. We need our friends in all sorts of different ways. We need them to share our interests, to share a joke with (I am sure if you asked most British people the most important thing they share with their friends the answer would be a sense of humour!), and to share our personal history. Friends who go 'way back' have become part of our story and part of our identity. We need to know there is someone on whom we can rely to accept us as we are, with whom we do not need to pretend or put on an act, and with whom we share our crises as well as our fun. We need to know that there is someone for whom we can do things, someone to whom we matter, someone who is simply grateful that we are around. For any married person the majority of those needs will be met by their partner; for the single person those basic human emotional needs will be met by our friends.

The other side of those needs has to be a recognition that we actually do not have rights over our friends. We have no right to depend completely on a friend, or to demand anything from them. No one friend can be a marriage partner substitute. Expecting too much of a friendship, and particularly asserting those expectations publicly, is another way of killing it stone dead. I once knew a friendship where one copied the other slavishly in dress, constantly called at her home, almost tried to become that person. It was a strange thing to witness – one attempting to become a clone of the other. It must have been the most awful claustrophobic experience for the one who was being copied and indeed she eventually moved some distance away. The single person who has accepted the projected view that she or he is inadequate as they are must be particularly prone to this sort of bizarre search for another, although in this case it was really a search to be a different person. It does not work. The only way to find contentment is to accept who you are, to accept your circumstances and to accept that if they need changing, there is only one person who can do that – you.

> I have no duty to be anyone's Friend and no man in the world has a duty to be mine.[15]

One of the great freedoms of the single life is the freedom to choose our friends. They are not inherited by a marriage ceremony and they are not restricted by anyone else's opinion. For that reason there is probably less pressure to have friends of a similar age – we discover the freedom to follow shared interests. C. S. Lewis has a clearly defined view of friendship in his book *The Four Loves*. Any female reader these days will grind her teeth over what he has to say about friendships between women, but the model of friendship he suggests, as two people side by side engaged in a common interest, is valid for either sex. We go out and do things with our friends, whether it is sport or attending plays or concerts or going to an exhibition. We do not, as lovers do, simply look to each other – we look to our enthusiasms.

There is therefore no reason why an age gap should be a problem, and for anyone in a lively church community there are a range of people with whom we can share our enthusiasms. It really does not matter if they are 40 years older!

The bereaved and the separated or divorced will

find single people less of a threat than married people. We are not reminding them constantly of what they have lost. We have had to face aspects of being alone and we can be a real help to those who find themselves suddenly plunged into that state, not by barging in and telling them, but by the way we live. Anyone who shows that life on your own is viable will present a glimmer of hope to those who feel that their own lives have ended with another's death. This has to be handled sensitively because no-one who has suffered loss needs someone else presenting themselves as the ideal model. Nonetheless it is a gift which single people have been given and which they can share.

Can there be true friendship between those of the opposite sex? C. S. Lewis assumes not, in his description of friendship: men are men and women are women, and the twain can meet only as lovers or possibly as colleagues. One has to resist a strong urge to hurl the book across the room. My own experience is that friendships are entirely possible when the boundaries are clearly set. So with married friends there is no problem, as long as there is an awareness of the possibility of creating jealousy. If there is any suggestion that the relationship could change then a withdrawal or cooling-off time might be necessary. It is always simplest to say these things straightaway rather than letting them fester, and certainly it is imperative to remain aware of your own motives. If you are drifting into the 'I would make a much better partner for him/her' syndrome, then stop kidding yourself that this is an ordinary friendship. Feelings can creep up on us unawares but as soon as we get an inkling of what is happening we need to act on it. Any wife or husband who feels that a single friend is monopolizing their spouse's time or energies has every reason to be jealous. So the rule is to remain vigilant about your own feelings and sensitive to those of others. Some misguided people regard all single people as a threat to others' marriages – but it is shattering to realize that you have fallen into the trap of becoming that threat yourself. Sometimes these situations come upon us quite unexpectedly, and the ability to stand back and see what we are doing when we are in the midst of it all is a rare gift. But all friendships have the potential to develop and change, and it would be downright stupid to avoid friendships with members of the opposite sex just in case things became uncomfortable! All our relationships, if they are to count for anything at all, carry an element of risk.

Personally, some of my deepest and most important friendships are with gay men. The parameters are already set, the rules are defined, and we can enjoy each other's company with no threat on either side. To be a balanced human being I need male company and from Gertrude Lawrence and Noel Coward onwards (and probably long before) gay men have needed the company of an uncomplicated woman who is not going to have designs on them. I have found that there are many parallels between my life and the lives of my gay male friends and that there are many interests in common. Experiences will often be similar – many gay men have to run their own homes, choose their own furnishings, go to social functions alone. While gay relationships remain unsanctioned by society at large and by the church in particular, single women who are aware of the situation can be of real help. With all the difficulties that are imposed on gay relationships a sympathetic, empathetic ear is always valuable. Single people know what it is like not to have total security in a relationship. But it is important to remain honest with yourself, and again, if you become aware that your own feelings are changing, then action needs to be taken.

The biggest risk of having feelings of friendship changing into something quite different is with heterosexual and unattached friends of the opposite sex. This may of course be a very good thing! Sometimes, though, it is inappropriate and another effective way of killing off a friendship is by developing an unrequited passion.

It can be very difficult, maybe even impossible, to control feelings, but sometimes we have to decide whether we value a friendship too much to risk losing it for the sake of a possible romantic attachment. Perhaps it is worth bearing in mind that all romance eventually dies, whether to be transformed into a firmer and more mature married love, or to dissipate into nothing, whereas friendships can last a lifetime.

Not all situations turn out as happily as they do in the pages of romantic fiction. In the film *When Harry Met Sally*, two people who have been friends for some years and have valued their platonic relationship find that they have fallen in love (not without a few hiccups of course, to make it interesting) and they get married. All very pleasant – but sometimes real life is less ideal, and for some single people life can be a long string of painful emotional upheavals.

> The Gospels show [Jesus] as one who had this gift of being friends with a wide variety of people.[16]

So far I have been talking about established friendships. What do you do, though, if you need friends and just do not have them? The situation can arise when you move to a new area or when other friends move away. Someone going out and searching for friends has a tough task ahead of them and if the need for friendship becomes obvious it can have the effect of frightening off all comers! When I began teaching I lived in a place where I knew no-one else and I had no idea how to start meeting people. I had come straight from university and college where I had a selection of possible friends ever before me. It was a big shock to find no such selection and to be told by one of my new colleagues that 'We don't like to socialize here'. In the end, but not before a period of shattering loneliness, I just had to move.

I would not now move to a place where I did not have at least a few contacts. People stronger than me might be able to manage it but I could not. Before making any moves for a job, it is important to consider how confidently you can view being in a new place alone. A married friend who had to move away for the sake of his job, returning at weekends to his wife and family, found that it takes quite literally years to become established somewhere new. Making friends from cold is not easy.

Usually the easiest way to make contact with possible friends is through work or church – the people we are thrown together with on a regular basis. If either of these two is an unfriendly place there will be difficulties, but it is possible to join a group, to develop other links, whether it is a sports club or music group or evening class. It has to be something you are genuinely interested in yourself, though, otherwise the whole idea of finding friends with whom you have something in common will fall to the ground! Always ask yourself before getting involved and committing time whether it is something you would want to do if you were not feeling friendless. There is no point in having something which you do not really enjoy taking up all your time, so that you will not be able to take other opportunities when they arise.

Go in peace, for we have sworn friendship with each other in the name of the Lord.[17]

The classic picture of a friendship in the Bible is that between David and Jonathan. Jonathan, we are told, became 'one in spirit with David'; he gave him many gifts, he stood up for him against King Saul, his powerful father. He quite literally risked life and limb for him, when Saul flung a spear at his son in his rage with David. Some of us might feel that this all seems a little one-sided and that Jonathan is one of those people with a dog-like devotion to his friend, but David's grief over Jonathan's death is very strongly expressed: 'You were very dear to me. Your love for me was wonderful, more wonderful than that of women.'[18] This is not necessarily evidence of a homosexual relationship, though it is not inconceivable that such a thing existed. It is David's recognition of Jonathan's sacrificial commitment to him. The most important thing that Jonathan did for David was to help him to find strength in God. He saw God at work throughout their friendship. At best, this is what friendship should always show us. We should learn from our friends something about ourselves, about other people and about God. Of course friendship groups can deteriorate and become mutual back-scratching circles. Of course they can be used to wield power – only look at some playground friendships and the way that a weaker or non-conforming child can be squeezed out. There is always the potential for any such group to work in the wrong way. But real friends, friendships that have been cemented by time and shared experiences, are a great gift. They do not just shield us from the unpleasant fact of our own aloneness; they add great richness to our lives.

They remind us that however isolated we might

feel, we are all linked by the 'golden cord close-binding all mankind'.[19] We are affected by each other's sadness or happiness, by each other's moods. We support each other and suffer with each other; we are involved with one another's lives.

Our friends remind us that we are all interconnected, at a time in the late 20th century when society feels disconnected. They restore to us that basic sense of being part of something, 'a piece of the continent, a part of the main'.[20] They remind us that we affect society, and that if we allow ourselves to slip into isolation we will be contributing to the dark heart of loneliness in that society. As Christians we are told to love one another, and it is through our friendships that we learn how to do that, how to love someone who is not our own flesh and blood. In our friends we learn about the love which flows through all who are connected to Christ. Of course these friendships are not exclusive to single people, but sometimes those who are married simply forget that they need other people and fail to keep their old friends or to make new ones.

When a married person is suddenly bereaved they sometimes find that they depended for all of their strength and security on that one person. If you are single you will already have learned something quite different, through your friendships. This is C. S. Lewis again: 'Christ, who said to the disciples, "Ye have not chosen me, but I have chosen you", can truly say to each group of Christian friends, "You have not chosen one another but I have chosen you for one another".' Through our friendships we will have learned about commitment, about self-giving, about love, about suffering, about shared jokes, about the sheer exuberant fact of being alive. We will have learned, in fact, rather a lot about God.

4

Love and sexuality

If I have a faith that can move mountains,
but have not love, I am nothing.[1]

There is a tendency in our society to interpret the word
'love' in any context as meaning romantic/erotic love
and to assume that we are indeed nothing without it.
You come across it all the time. You are incomplete
unless you are 'in a relationship'. You have really no
idea of true happiness. You should probably be hang-
ing your head in shame at the degradation. Without
obvious sexual fulfilment you will probably be an
emotional wreck, no matter how you try to hide it.

Advertisements obviously trade on this assumption. Buy enough exotic ice cream and everything in
your love life will blossom. Use the right body spray
and members of the opposite sex will be seized by an
irresistible urge to shove a bouquet of flowers into
your hands, with the inevitable romantic consequences.
Apply the correct deodorant and you will not only be
plunged into a life of passion; you will also find yourself transported somewhere tropical in the twinkling
of an eye – very erotic. Smouldering glances and exciting glimpses of tanned flesh sell products, it seems. I
suppose that there is no harm done if you buy the
products and reject the message, but if you accept the
message, things could be more difficult. If you have
swallowed the line that the only way to find fulfilment

in life is by finding a mate, you may well have a rude awakening when you do find one.

As Christians, we have a higher definition of love and of fulfilment. The statement by the House of Bishops, *Issues in Human Sexuality*, published in 1991, has this to say about the single life:

> No true disciple of Christ can accept the fashionable opinion of our times that experience of full physical sex relations is necessary for our fulfilment as human beings. Our Lord himself and many of his greatest saints have been living proof that this is not so.

It is far too easy to be swept along by society's view, to accept perhaps that without an active sex life we are inadequate human beings. Whatever magazine you open, whichever full and frank television programme you tune into, sexual pleasure is an essential human right and an end in itself. Perhaps, you can find yourself thinking, I am an inadequate human being. Perhaps I should be yearning to jump into bed with a variety of partners. Am I repressed, am I undersexed, am I such a closet gay that even I haven't realized it? Am I the only person in the world who thinks it's a good idea to get to know someone well before contemplating having sex with them? Where does love and commitment come in? You have to keep reminding yourself that you do not have to accept that pressure from society, that there are different values, and that to work out those values for yourself is not repressive but liberating.

We are each valued as unique individuals by God and are free to work out with God's guidance our own morality, freed from the sexual mores of our times. Looking to the Church for answers is not always instructive, particularly if we accept the media's interpretation of what the Church is saying. Somehow we have to steer a course between the prevailing view that a complete human being explores every avenue of genital sex in a search for individual satisfaction, and the opposing one that the only safe way is to avoid any temptations to lustful behaviour. Between these two extremes there are many permutations and everyone will have different needs and reactions. We are all sexual beings, but we vary enormously in our sexual appetites and in our views of how, or if, those appetites should be met.

Most people would acknowledge that there are certain appetites which certainly should not be met, where another person will be hurt or become emotionally damaged or where children are involved. But in the general range of sexual activity it is our individual conscience which comes into play, in the Christian's case informed by prayer. The Church does not necessarily lay down hard and fast rules for behaviour, even whilst stating particular ideals. We may well know within our own church communities single mothers, gay people in committed relationships, couples living together; all sorts of people who have not accepted the 'traditional' Christian view of sexual morality.

It is clear that most Christians do not regard promiscuity as an option and that faithfulness and commitment must be key elements of any relationship. Ultimately, though, we must decide for ourselves what sort of life we will lead, and for the single Christian that may be a responsible exploring of intimate relationships, a life of chastity, or even a commitment to celibacy.

True love is not a feeling by which we are overwhelmed. It is a committed, thoughtful decision.[2]

Deep inside most of us there lurks a yearning to play the romantic lead, to be swept off our feet by a grand passion. Who has not at one time or another seen themselves in a 'Cathy' or 'Heathcliff' role, rushing headlong over the moor and leaving all lesser beings behind in the white heat of passion? Well, me actually; I've never been a fan of the Brontës, but you get the idea. Romantic melodrama! Love stories are always a hot topic, monopolizing more time than any other emotion in TV soaps and song lyrics, crowding the bookstalls, grabbing the headlines. Even *The Archers* (to the disgust of some of its followers) is periodically taken over by the love interest. It is an extraordinary obsession.

We do not choose when we are going to love. We feel it in many different contexts and in all sorts of different relationships. It cuts through all our sophistication and leaves us open and vulnerable. It moves us to tears and sometimes to anger. It is at the centre of our lives as Christians, the love of God searing through the most dreary situations. At no time is it limited to the soupy romantic context and as most happily married couples will tell you, when the soupy romance has gone, it is the true love which remains. We feel it for our family, friends, pets, gardens .... I even feel it, on a good day, for my class!

The question is, do single people experience love with the same intensity as married people do? It would be ridiculous for me to claim that I have the same experience of love, because if I never have that particular relationship with one other person then of course life will be different. But most of us will have fallen in love at some time in our lives; many of us will feel that our hearts have been broken and we have had to spend a period of time in mending them. One of the possibilities – or probabilities – to be faced after that is that you will never be loved by one person alone, you will never be another's 'special person'. If you are at a time of life when everyone around you seems to have a special person, when even your closest friends get married (how dare they?), then there is no denying that it hurts. I do not think I have ever felt so alone as I did when one of my closest friends was married – suddenly it was just me on my own and it felt like the world was full of happy couples. Add to that a broken relationship of your own, or difficulties at work, and there is an instant fit of depression.

But while time almost certainly does not heal all wounds, it makes most of them easier to cope with and makes us more realistic. Once the rose-tinted specs are off, it becomes painfully apparent that some of those partnerships we had envied are actually far from enviable. Our assumption that everyone was going to live happily ever after (with the notable exception of ourselves) is seen to be sadly untrue. I have to say that many marriages make me extremely glad to be single.

So what about love? It is a basic necessity of life to love and to be loved. Can single people experience that? Once you have cleared the romantic garbage out of your concept of love ('The myth of romantic love is a dreadful lie', to quote M. Scott Peck), the answer is yes, of course. Anyone who works with children experiences it all the time. I was once sitting on the floor with my class during a school assembly when I was moved to tears by an older child's solo. As I surreptitiously wiped my eyes, a small hand crept into mine, to comfort me. If that is not love, what is it? Love is open to all of us, as long as we do not try to live in a vacuum.

Take the talent from him and give it to the one who

has the ten talents. For everyone who has will be given more, and he will have an abundance.[3]

There is a lot of sentimental claptrap written about love, notably on greetings cards and in cheap verse, but the fact remains that love is our chief talent to use. Whenever we love we take risks, we lay ourselves open to rejection. True love expects nothing in return: the much maligned Quasimodo in Victor Hugo's novel *Notre Dame de Paris* (now there is a sad single person, if you are looking for one to feel sorry for) protects the heroine, risks his life to save her, and in the end dies for her and gets nothing at all in return. So often we think of love as something we receive, but the truth of the gospel shows us that the greatest part is the giving of love as Jesus gave it in his life and in his death.

The ability to love is a gift given to each of us, a talent that will not profit much by being buried. No single person can afford to sit at home bemoaning a lack of love. We have to get out and *do* it. In the words of St John of the Cross, 'Pour in love where there is no love and you'll draw love out.' Some of the most loving people I know are single, from members of religious communities to celibate priests, to a single friend at my own church who was the mother figure to generations of Brownies!

She said she hoped to see me some day with a number of children about me, my own children. Never, I said, adding I did not believe that I should ever marry. Then came out by degrees my attachment to C.[4]

If you have read the Reverend Robert Francis Kilvert's diary you will know how desperate the poor man was to marry, how susceptible to the charms of the ladies and how, sadly, he died just one month after his marriage.

The search for a marriage partner can become an obsession for some, an overwhelming need. Without their supposed 'other half' they feel without value. It is wrong, of course, but how can you ever stop yourself feeling it?

Not being married does hurt even the best-adjusted single person sometimes. When I am asked to attend a social event 'with partner' or when I have to correct someone who has written 'Mrs' before my name, I must confess to feeling a pang. Society expects people my age to be married (pretty stupid, really, when you think how many are not). The parent of one of the children in my class cross-questioned my classroom assistant as to why I was not married with children. Good heavens, with all my experience of teaching them, motherhood would be a cinch, she thought. Well, not having children does hurt and goes on hurting – it will hurt, no doubt, when I have no grandchildren of my own. Undoubtedly the experience of childbirth can be a great spiritual experience and the seeing of oneself in another must be intensely pleasurable. There are, though, many opportunities when our parenting instincts can be used. Most parents I know are only too pleased to lend their children out for a day (more, if they can get away with it). We do not have to exist in a child-free environment (though there are some days when I yearn for such a Utopia) and we do not have to be biological parents to be loved by children. Not having a long term sexual relationship and not having children has left a gap in my life but lots of people live with gaps, and some with much worse ones. Nothing is going to fill the gap and there is no magic wand to be waved. Despite the assertions of some prominent evangelists, God does not always provide what we think we need. Some things in life we just have to live with – or live without.

This may provide evidence clear to any outsider that I am an obvious candidate for a celibate life. Perhaps the very fact that I can happily accept my life as it is shows that I would not be very good at it if it were different. Certainly I have known people who were driven by a longing to find a partner, as Kilvert was, to whom the sight of any married couple opened up deep wounds, who would go to any lengths to find a mate. For me personally, the idea of dating agencies or any other form of arranged meetings is complete anathema. It is bad enough when friends contrive a meeting – nothing is more guaranteed to render my behaviour eccentric or my demeanour that of a frightened rabbit. Others may well be murmuring 'what a wimp', or 'some of the happiest couples I know met through that reputable agency The Jolly Soulmate Christian Dating Service.' Well, murmur as you will, I know what I am capable of. And that really is the key to it. If you are sure of your own needs and your own capabilities then you will know whether it is appropriate for you to pull out all the stops in the search for the man or woman of your dreams, or whether you would really rather not. An older friend of mine, looking back on her life, remarked, 'I think I was too lazy to bother looking for a husband really. I was busy with lots of other things and it all seemed too much effort.' The evidence is there to see now: she is a very happy and fulfilled person, active and involved with all sorts of aspects of church and community life, perfectly content not to have had a husband.

Without thinking highly either of men or of matrimony, marriage had always been her object; it was the only honourable provision for well-educated young women of small fortune and, however uncertain of giving happiness, must be their pleasantest preservative from want.[5]

We no longer live in a society where marriage offers the only escape from the parental home but there can still be a great deal of social pressure to marry. For some people the pressure will arise as part of their job, something which clergy are particularly subject to. How many parishes in their search for a new vicar ask for a 'family person'? Marriage equals being settled down and sensible (ha!). Family expectations too can make you feel hounded – families love a good wedding and can be quite put out when one member will not buckle down and give them one! One of my aunts, with great kindness, allowed me to have first choice of my grandmother's rings ... 'as you don't have an engagement ring of your own'. It was one of those occasions when I gritted my teeth, bit back the retort, and then chose the one I liked best. After all, I don't have an engagement ring, do I? If the misguided choose to feel sorry for me, who am I to deny them the pleasure?

I really am grateful to be living in a culture and a time when arranged marriages are not the norm. Having seen the upheaval that an Asian friend has had to go through in her family's search for a husband for her, any ideas that it might be an easy answer are soon dispelled. As to giving in to the pressure which exists in contemporary British culture, it really is a question of how much you want to be married. My own feeling has always been that if the ideal man walked into my life then I am not silly enough to send him packing, but, on the other hand, life is too short to waste my time looking for him. I am certainly not prepared, and no-one should be, to compromise for the sake of being married. Sadly, people do it all the time. 'I can't possibly be left on the shelf' is the feeling. Some women marry in haste to be sure of having children. Others find themselves getting married because all the rest of their set were 'settling down'. There is a lurking fear of being left out, being the one people will feel sorry for. Well, no-one needs to feel sorry for the single person unless they show themselves worthy of pity.

There is a wonderfully funny scene in the novel *Crampton Hodnet* by Barbara Pym in which the curate, having decided that he 'might do worse than marry Miss Morrow', proposes marriage to her. She should be grateful; she is a paid companion and he is offering her an escape. She is shrewd enough to see that it is a compromise all the way along the line. It came into his mind purely as a way of altering the drudgery of his life, and the episode ends by his looking ridiculous, as all who propose marriage as an escape should. Fortunately, Miss Morrow is more sensible: 'Hasn't it occurred to you,' she says, 'you would soon find yourself wanting to escape from a marriage to a woman you didn't love?' He pursues it a bit further:

'You don't seem to realise that one can learn to care', said Mr Latimer pompously. 'No I don't', said Miss Morrow firmly. 'Learning to care always seems to me to be one of the most difficult lessons that can be imagined. How does one set about it? Perhaps we might do it together, like Russian, in the long winter evenings?'

There is no point at all in getting married to make yourself feel loved or accepted. There is no point at all in hoping that someone else will change your life. A marriage like that could be a trap and, as Miss Morrow says, 'how much more difficult that would be than just finding new lodgings!' If your life is not right, you are the one who must change it, not just wait to be rescued.

Stories of knights on white chargers and beautiful

damsels in distress tend to end with the first kiss. You do not hear about how he turned out to be an opinionated bore and how she longed for the excitement of life with the dragon. Actually we do not usually need someone else to rescue us; we can do it ourselves. Change is possible in most situations, as long as the will to change is there. As Christians we are promised change, fulfilment, a new life: 'Therefore, if anyone is in Christ, he is a new creation; the old has gone, the new has come!'[6] It may well be that changes will be affected by new relationships, but to look for a relationship to do that is shortsighted and probably doomed to failure.

> Do you think, she said, that true love can exist between a woman and a man, if the woman feels more and more every day that she wants to hit the man over the head with a brick?[7]

Most people are at their most attractive when they are not actively seeking a mate. There is something positively repellent about the classic frustrated female or sex-starved male. That predatory look in the eye, the slightly frantic attempts at fascinating conversation, the inappropriate grabbing of portions of the anatomy, make most people beat a hasty retreat. Memories of being trapped by any such afflicted person tend to remain vivid. I remember having to listen to boastful accounts of sporting/business/academic prowess, which were supposed to bowl me over and instead gave me a strong urge to go home and read a book. At one ghastly party I was cornered by a Morris dancer who insisted on showing me all the steps, alluringly. Awful, isn't it? We've all been there. Some of us may even have demonstrated Morris-dancing steps. The trouble is that when we try to be enticing, we all too often appear repulsive.

These things are easy to see with the benefit of hindsight and it is undeniable that when we are in the middle of one of those periods of feeling the need for a mate, it is very difficult not to show it! Age and experience help, of course, but it is nevertheless one of the facts of most single people's lives that they will go through periods of feeling that they really must find a partner.

Even worse are those infatuations (if you have never felt these and are feeling superior, you are a rare bird indeed) which you can recognize on one level but on another find almost impossible to control. Anyone, it seems, is prone to these – even Bertie Wooster's Uncle George, 'The last bloke in the world, in short, who you would think would ever fall a victim to the divine pash'[8] – and very uncomfortable they can be. You know you are being ridiculous, but how do you control that quickening of the pulse or the tell-tale blush? There is always the lingering romantic fantasy that, after all, this might be The One. Well, it is always possible but all too often you are left with egg on your face.

One of the impulses to guard against is the strong urge to try to bully God into giving you what you think you want. 'Just give me so-and-so Lord and I'll be happy.' 'I'm sure he's very keen really Lord, just arrange the romantic finale.' A useful prayer to use in those times when you just are not sure of what to think or what to do is the simple, 'Spirit of truth, lead me into the way of all truth.' It is a great way to cut through all the balderdash you have been kidding yourself with and getting back in touch with reality.

> That's what brings happiness, a moment-by-moment contact with reality. That's where you'll find God.[9]

We can only live with what we have now, with the life that we have now, rather than constantly looking for something 'better'. Accepting your present situation means a great liberation, the realization that you do not have to view every new acquaintance as a potential partner. The reality is that we are all made in God's image and that you are who you are, not by virtue of the way that you respond to one particular person, your 'mate', but by virtue of the way that you respond to God.

Singleness is sometimes seen as a denial of sexuality but it need be nothing of the sort. We do not depend on another person to feel male or female; we depend on ourselves. Gender issues – male or female, gay or straight – help to define who we are. We need to fully accept our sexuality and our feelings if we are to be healthy human beings. There are some strange ideas about this in some church circles, particularly on the extreme end of the deliverance ministry movement. Without wishing to tar all who are involved in Christian healing with this extremist brush, single people must be aware that sexual urges do not require healing. The poor young man who was reported to have had consecrated Ribena poured down his underpants to cleanse him of lustful thoughts[10] could surely have found a better outlet for his feelings, and without the laundry problems.

Any psychologist will tell you that a feeling denied is a feeling that will emerge in a much more dangerous form – and psychologists can be Christians too. We need to acknowledge fantasies (which I am capable of having at the most inappropriate times and places) and feelings of sexual attraction. What you do with those feelings is up to you, but the important thing is not to deny their existence. Sexual feelings are as strong if not stronger than most other feelings and they have to be admitted to if they are going to be manageable.

71

Undoubtedly one of the difficulties of being single is working out how to express oneself physically and with whom. There is a real need for physical contact in all of us. In my job physical contact is built in with children turning to me for reassurance, which is best expressed towards the very young and perhaps the not-so-young by touch. Even that is open to misinterpretation, as a number of court cases against teachers have shown. One of the things that any single person has to work out is when it is safe to touch and be touched and how far a friendly hug can go. That is something which can only be explored by individuals, and there are certainly no hard and fast rules, but it is essential to review one's own attitudes and feelings.

There are certainly times when we need to be hugged and need the friends who can do the hugging. I remember feeling this quite desperately when I'd had to attend a child's funeral with my headteacher, who was not the sort of person to dish out hugs to his staff. My need had to be stored up until I was able to go round to see a friend later. There are times when we simply have to feel another person's arms around us in order to come to terms with something that has happened. Touch at a time like that says more than a thousand words can possibly do.

If you do not have a relationship in your life already where it is 'safe' to touch, then it is not something you can just switch on, but it is worth exploring tentatively with a friend. Even a touch on the hand or an arm around the shoulders can help enormously, breaking down that feeling of isolation.

Sometimes the need for a physical expression of sexuality becomes quite overwhelming and then some might find that masturbation is the answer for them. Others would not find any satisfaction in it or indeed might have a great deal of guilt about it. One thing I have discovered in the past few months is that it is a very difficult subject to discuss with other people because nothing ends a conversation more effectively than a question about sex, especially the sort involving one person only. (No-one would ever employ me on one of those late-night 'no holds barred' sex programmes on Channel 4.)

Masturbation is seen as an embarrassing topic and no-one is ever keen to admit to it, but whether there should really be any guilt attached to it is quite another matter. What is worth mentioning is that it is by no means a necessary consequence of being single, and indeed could just as easily be a way of dealing with difficulties in a married relationship.

Being feminine or masculine, however, goes much deeper than deciding what to do with our genitals. It is expressed through our dress, through the way we may do our hair and all of those superficial things, but it is expressed more strongly in the ways in which we think and in which we view the world. If you have any doubts about this, try visiting two religious communities, one male and one female. They will have, I guarantee, a completely different atmosphere. 'Male and female he created them', as it says in Genesis 1. There are undoubtedly books, films and any number of activities which will appeal to one sex more than the other. We are different, even with all our similarities.

Sexuality is one of those ever lively topics of gossip – few of us can say that we have never, with a few boon companions, had a 'well, do you think he's gay?' conversation. It is one of those things that people do enjoy speculating about; we have only to look at the prurient gossip that is stirred up by the 'Outrage' group when they decide to 'out' a well-known figure, or the immense pleasure derived from any political sex scandal. Unfortunately, any single person has to accept that questions will undoubtedly be being asked about their sexual orientation. It can be difficult to come to terms with being thought other than you are, because no matter how liberal your views may be, your sexuality is an essential part of you. As the House of Bishops' report, *Issues in Human Sexuality* (1991) says, 'We are men or women in everything we do, and we should enjoy the colour and delight, the strength and sensitivity this brings and which is one of God's loveliest gifts.'

How do we value that gift? First of all, I suppose, by taking a pride in our appearance. I always feel nervous when a conversation gets round to someone who has 'let themselves go', as I am not sure that I ever had myself in hand. But it is not just to do with the careful application of eye make-up or whatever the masculine equivalent might be. It is about remembering to get your hair cut and thinking about what clothes you are going to put on, rather than crawling about looking unkempt, a ragbag of jumble sale cast-offs. Your opinion of yourself shows in your appearance. Most of us can tell at a glance when someone has just ceased to believe in themselves as a reasonable human being. Secondly, you can value that gift by conversations at a deep level with people of the same sex, by discovering all those things that are held in common. And finally, you can value it by acknowledging how attractive you find the opposite sex – after all, according to Genesis 2, we were made for each other!

> Be thou as chaste as ice, as pure as snow, thou shalt
> not escape calumny.[11]

Chastity has almost become a joke word in our culture. Mention chastity belts and you get an easy laugh. Chastity is thought of as being the sole preserve of nuns and (snigger, snigger) that is only because they

have never met a 'real' man. If you have thought
through your choices and decided that you cannot
choose sex outside marriage then you have, for the
moment, chosen chastity. Shout that from the mountain tops and you will soon get laughed down.
Chastity is not popular. It certainly was not always like
that – until very recently it was the 'respectable' way
to behave. Such is the roller coaster of social attitudes,
just now we are in a very different phase, no matter
how hard the politicians may shout for a 'return to
family values'.

In the Christian Church and within most other
religions, abstaining from sexual relations is still a
virtue. From the prophet Jeremiah onwards, the idea
of a person who is dedicated to God having no truck
with sex has been a very central idea. John the Baptist,
Jesus himself, St Paul and countless Christian people
through the centuries have chosen chastity. St Paul has
no doubt at all about it – 'I wish that all men were as I
am.'[12] On the other hand, 'If they cannot control
themselves, they should marry, for it is better to marry
than to burn with passion.'[13]

If you have for the moment chosen chastity, then
you must recognize that it does not actually make you
any more virtuous than anyone else – doing without
something does not necessarily help to build the
Kingdom! If you think that this path must include the
rejection of any sexual feelings, then you have really
got your work cut out. It seems to me that to thank
God for those feelings which remind us of our sexuality and help us to keep in touch with our humanity is
a much more practical way forward. Why suffer a
burden of guilt for what is, after all, an entirely normal
reaction?

Not everyone can accept this teaching, but only

those to whom it has been given. For some are eunuchs because they were born that way; others were made that way by men; and others have renounced marriage because of the kingdom of heaven. The one who can accept this should accept it.[14]

So if you have chosen to be chaste, does that make you celibate? Celibacy is one of those things that is creeping in as a backlash to the sexual revolution and gaining rather more credence as prominent people like the actor Stephen Fry publicly espouses it. Celibacy is not something which occurs by default; it is a particular gift, which enables the celibate to dedicate him- or herself to God's work. Paul's idea that 'An unmarried woman or virgin is concerned about the Lord's affairs: Her aim is to be devoted to the Lord in both body and spirit'[15] may not ring quite true for some who have had the single life thrust upon them! A spiritual adviser may suggest to a single person that they may be being led to a celibate life, but no earthly person can attach the label to you if it is not one that you can hear God calling you to accept. As a Christian calling, celibacy is something quite different. It is not something which you can choose for yourself; it is something which God has chosen for you.

This does not mean, of course, that the person who is called to celibacy will find it an easy path or that suddenly all those yearnings and longings will be switched off. What it does do is to give a clearer purpose to the single life – freeing the person concerned from any 'if only' thoughts. Even then it need not be a lifelong calling, as the experiences of those religious suddenly called to marriage show!

It is a calling that can be tested – some people decide to make a short-term commitment, often with the support of a Christian community. You do not have to join a religious order to try it out! What is clear is that it should never be chosen as a way of running away to escape your own feelings; as Jonah found, God has a way of finding out those who try to run away. Somehow, in Paul's words, 'Each of you should learn to control his own body in a way that is holy and honourable',[16] and that means asking God which way is right for you.

> Understand that maybe you've got the wrong ideas and it is these ideas that are influencing your life and making it the mess that it is and keeping you asleep. Ideas about love, ideas about freedom, ideas about happiness and so forth.[17]

It is all too easy to accept someone else's projected view of you, to decide that you are unloved or that you must be unfulfilled. No-one – least of all someone who is single and has to work it out for themselves – can afford to do that. We cannot rely on the second-hand in our lives or in our emotions. We cannot accept someone else's beliefs, whether they are of a spiritual or moral nature, to get us through life. Recently someone told me, 'Don't leave it too late to get married.' (I hadn't hitherto realized that I had a queue of suitors to choose from.) 'You are missing out on one of the greatest joys of life.' Well, with the greatest respect, how does he know what the greatest joy of my life might be? Fulfilment comes for many people through a happy marriage and children. For others, a marriage can be a painful experience and bringing up children can be a tough business. Fulfilment comes from the happy acceptance of what life brings to us and for some that will not include marriage, ever.

Corrie ten Boom, in her book *The Hiding Place*, tells the moving story of her sister's wholehearted embracing of the admonition to 'Give thanks in all circumstances'.[18] Few of us could give thanks for the fleas which infested the sleeping quarters in a Nazi concentration camp – but it was those very fleas which kept the guards out and which gave the prisoners freedom of worship. Giving thanks for what we have, including the very thing which we think is our greatest burden, may well be the key to personal fulfilment. Of course, there will be things we cannot do, experiences we have not had, those gaps in our lives – but there are few who have no gaps at all!

If we look at the life of the person whom Christians would regard as the most perfectly fulfilled, we cannot help but notice that, actually, he was single too. Jesus' life was full of people, friends and love. He encountered people from all levels of society, of either sex and of any age. He did not have to stay at home looking after the family – in fact, he posed that hard question, 'Who is my mother, and who are my brothers?'[19] He did not have to prove his sexuality to gain the heartfelt respect, not just of his followers but also of virtually everyone he came in contact with. He was obviously free to cry, to laugh, to touch and to embrace. He was able to show compassion to a woman who was suffering a haemorrhage, which no respectable Jewish man should ever have done – and to respond without anger to her touch. He was free to gather children to him, to socialize with the socially unacceptable, to show a capacity for deep friendships with men and women. He did all of this not because he was using his divinity to shield himself, but because he used his humanity to make himself completely open – 'He opened wide his arms for us on the cross'.[20]

Our response to those open arms will make all the difference in the world and it is there that we will find true fulfilment.

5

The Church community

> Now you are the body of Christ, and each
> one of you is a part of it.[1]

One of the basic truths of the Christian life, and one
which we are most liable to forget, is that every person's calling and every person's response to God is an
individual one. We are each of us answerable to God
not as part of a marriage or a family, or even a terribly
nice church in West London, or wherever, but as ourselves. We are all, in that sense, single. Our Christian
community can support us, help us to grow spiritually,
look after us in old age or in sickness, provide a social
group and do any number of other things, but there
has to be a personal commitment and a personal faith
or we would not be Christians.

Yet there are still some churches where you get the
distinct feeling that single people are not really part of
the community and where a single person can feel
excluded by the prayers, the preaching, the social
events and by individual reactions. No children to bring
along to Sunday School, no partner to accompany you
to the Harvest barn dance, no family for the family
service. What on earth are you doing in our 'family'
church?

In some churches there will be an even more
extreme attitude to the single state, with the men
being under very real pressure to marry and the

women expected to come under the headship of the pastor, in the absence of a husband as head. One friend had the experience of being told exactly that (a dangerous position for any church leader to take up these days), and after she and other women were also asked to cover their heads as a sign of their submission, she left.

The fact is that a third of all church members are single so that, as a recent report by the General Synod Board for Social Responsibility says, 'The overwhelming emphasis in our culture on "coupledom" has to be resisted.'[2] Resisting that tendency has to mean positive moves to affirm those who are single and will certainly entail correcting the picture of the ideal family with which we are so often presented. That correction will be of obvious benefit to the single people in the congregation – especially those who are not happy to be on their own – but would also help the many church members whose family lives or marriages are so stressful that the church may be their only solace. The last thing that anyone with a difficult home life needs is for the church to present an idealized happy family picture, making their own lives feel like failure. As any single person knows, there are certain stress points during the year – Christmas, Mothering Sunday, bank holidays – when one's own solitary state can seem unbearable. Churches, which should value each member and affirm individual differences, can all too often appear harshly judgemental and exclusive. The very community which should be a haven of loving acceptance can feel like a source of unhappiness and instil an inappropriate feeling of inadequacy.

The problem is not so much one of real prejudice as of inaccurate assumptions being made. It is those assumptions that hurt. It is assumed that anyone of a certain age will be married, that that marriage will be happy, and, conversely, that if we are single, it must be a problem. A church which wishes to tackle those assumptions must be prepared to do so actively, enabling its members to express feelings and being quite daring in its approach. There are times when this will mean breaking a well-established pattern of social events to make them more inclusive. It may mean taking a long, hard look at the ways in which we use language, and it may mean directly challenging the assumptions through preaching.

> One sure sign of an inadequate set of social and moral values is the tendency to see singleness as a problem, or a failure to reach the ideal of a sexual partnership or 'married bliss'.[3]

All of this seems a far cry from St Paul's discourses on the single life in 1 Corinthians: 'Now to the unmarried . . . I say, it is good for them to stay unmarried, as I am.'[4] Paul saw marriage as a distraction from getting on with the Lord's business, a real problem for anyone seriously committed to their faith. The first and greatest commandment, after all, is to 'love the Lord your God with all your heart and with all your soul and with all your mind.'[5] The search for an individual relationship with God, freed from the distractions of other relationships, once sent hermits out into the desert and anchorites into solitude and there are still those who feel called to the isolation of a hermit's life. It really is time that the single life was given real value by all Church communities, a 'clear recognition that the single life is as valid as the married life'.[6]

The issue of marital status can be more troublesome for clergy than for their congregations – so many Christian groups looking for a new priest or minister will still be searching for a 'married man with children'. Single women can be perceived as unstable, single men may be of suspect sexuality; you are safe with a married man, or so it is thought (I have known some strange ones in my time, even so). It can go further than this, though – all sorts of constraints can be put on single clerics. If they keep themselves to themselves they are unsociable; if they socialize too much with certain members of the church they are said to have their favourites; if they accept all invitations for meals they are too lazy to cook for themselves; if they do not accept them they are stand-offish. I have even heard it said that they should not make friendships within their congregation – what a lonely existence! We all must have the right to choose our own friends, even those who lead semi-public lives, and there will be a particular need for them if we are single.

> Even the most intellectual of persons are seldom averse to gossip, though they may affect to despise it.[7]

Any close community – a village, a housing estate, a place of work, a church – will have an element of gossip in its working. Everyone does it, to a greater or a lesser extent, and everyone will at some time or another be the victim of it. Sometimes churches can be even more prone to gossip than other communities, particularly if there is that supposedly good-natured feeling of 'we thought you ought to know . . .'. Some single people may feel supported by people taking an interest in their lives, but it can get out of hand. Apparent concern can be busy-bodiness in a different guise and it is even true that a request for prayer for someone else can be a subtle way of passing on gossip. 'Do pray for so and so, she's going through a rough patch,' begs the question of what exactly the rough patch entails, and an offer of help can actually be a request for information. Moreover, the atmosphere of openness and sharing which exists in a good church community means that those who like to ask direct questions in order to extract a few interesting snippets can have a field day. It is essential to have set one's own parameters, to have decided how much of oneself one is willing to give away and not to be lulled into revealing too much. Information is power and there are not many church communities where one or two people are not playing power games, with significant looks, veiled references and carefully leaked juicy gossip items.

This may be beginning to sound like extreme paranoia on my part, but Dietrich Bonhoeffer, in his book on living in a Christian community, says this: 'To speak about a brother covertly is forbidden, even under the cloak of help and good will; for it is precisely in this guise that the spirit of hatred among brothers always creeps in when it is seeking to create mischief.'[8] He speaks of 'the Ministry of holding one's tongue' and I am sure that if only I could learn to practise that, life would be much easier! For any church community, vigilance about gossip is essential to protect the vulnerable – and most single people *are* vulnerable, like it or not.

A significant area of vulnerability is likely to be the well-meaning urge of fellow church members to marry off the single members, convinced that they are helping them on the path to happiness. There is something particularly galling about this urge, quite apart from the implied assumption that you cannot really do these things on your own. The intrusive questioning rises to new heights, from 'Are you and . . . courting, dear?' to 'Have you named the day yet?', accompanied by light and merry laughter, as if matters of the utmost privacy can and should be discussed at length with whoever happens to be wondering about it.

If the answer is truly, 'We are just good friends', it is given to few to accept that statement at face value. The trouble is that it takes some determination to go on pursuing an ordinary friendship in the face of such constant noseyness, and the well-meaning comments can kill a tentative relationship stone dead. Match-making should be banned from churches and the eagle-eyed gossip shot at dawn ... but meanwhile I would be content with a recognition that we all need good relationships with both sexes if we are to be balanced human beings.

> Aunt Wilma ... had black agate eyes that moved restlessly and scrutinized everybody with bright suspicion. In church, her glance would dart around the congregation seeking out irreverent men and women whose expressions showed they were occupied with worldly concerns, or even carnal thoughts, in the holy place.[9]

Mercifully, there are not too many Aunt Wilmas about these days and the flipside of the gossip peril is that there will be a number of people who do have a stake in your life, to whom you matter deeply, who will be willing and able to support you through any number of crises. From my own church I have gained a great deal of practical support as well as love and friendship and space for spiritual growth. I have learned how to gloss paint a door impeccably; I have received innumerable pieces of advice on car maintenance (not my strong point), and there are a number of listening ears to whom I know I can always turn.

The community to which I belong is an essential part of my life – and without it my life would be immeasurably poorer. Of course I am talking about a faith community, a group of people with whom I will automatically have certain things in common; but looking from a worldly point of view, I also have a buffer against being alone and a place where I am accepted. In our society there are many who do not have a wider community, whose security stops at their front doors, who have very few people whom they can trust. As an elderly single friend in my own church said, 'If you are single and lonely then you couldn't do better than to join a church; it's a sort of club where you can easily find friends.' Of course a church is more than a club – but that doesn't mean that its club aspect is to be despised!

For many single people their church may well be the centre of their social life; it is a place where common values can be found, where they can meet a variety of people of different ages and occupations, and where they can truly belong. It can be an important source of friends and provides a structure to the week. The latter point may well become particularly important with increasing age, when work is no longer providing a timetable. Church is something to give meaning to life, something to get up for in the mornings. I am not suggesting that this is the primary function of church membership, but it is certainly an important by-product. A church should be a place where people feel needed, involved and cared for, a place where they can look after others and be kept busy. 'Gainful employment' may sound old-fashioned, but it can give great satisfaction because, hackneyed as it might sound, we all need to feel useful, especially those of us who do not have partners or offspring demanding attention.

In his novel *A Clergyman's Daughter*, George Orwell portrays a sad woman, Dorothy, who loses her faith but in the end cannot give up her Christian way of life, this despite a period of memory loss when she lives rough on the streets of London and amongst hop-pickers in Kent. She cannot give it up for all it is derided by one of her new friends: 'The Girl Guides, the Mothers' Union, the Band of Hope, the Companionship of Marriage, parish visiting and Sunday School teaching, Holy Communion twice a week and here we go round the doxology-bush, chanting Gregorian plain-song'.[10] The Church had given meaning and shape to her existence and she simply could not live without it. For many single people (and for many who are not) it still has exactly that function.

But the Church has much more to offer than simply using up time. The communal aspect of involvement in a particular church, for example, can be immensely life-enhancing. Learning to share in the lives of others, to be involved in the practical day-to-day work of a church and worshipping together in the quiet mid-week services as well as the busyness of a Sunday all adds to the richness of our lives. It means far more than just being one of Barbara Pym's 'spinsters presiding over the tea urn'.[11] It means involvement in the church as *family*.

> What is known as a full life, with clergymen and jumble sales and church services and good works .... 'I thought that was the kind of life led by women who didn't have a full life in the accepted sense', said Helena.[12]

There are dangers, of course. There is the danger of simply going through the motions of being a Christian because there is no obvious alternative lifestyle; there is the danger of drifting along unthinkingly and using the church or using fellow-Christians and giving nothing in return. There is the danger of stopping at the having-a-good-time-together aspect and not seeking opportunities to grow spiritually. I well remember my university chaplain complaining crossly, 'This is a chaplaincy, not a social club!', which came as news to most of us. There is the danger of becoming exclusive, such a tight-knit group that no newcomer can get a toehold into it. There is the danger of staying in a church which we know is no longer right for us, simply because we cannot bear to leave our friends behind.

But Dietrich Bonhoeffer in *Life Together* has it right, I think, when he speaks of life within a Christian community as 'an unspeakable gift for the lonely individual'. No single person should cast that gift aside without really examining its value.

> We need to ask ourselves whether the Church always gives the same prayerful attention to the human and spiritual needs of single people as it commonly does to the married or those in the religious life.[13]

How often does a church committee settle down to debate the issue of serving the single members of the congregation? Compared with the debates on meeting the needs of young families or serving the teenagers, I should imagine that it is a pretty rare event. Most church leaders would assume that single people are just getting on with it and do not need special care. This is generally true . . . but there are certain instances when sensitivity to the needs of such a sizeable minority is essential. One such is Mothering Sunday. Over several years in my own church a bunch of daffodils was thrust into my hands at the morning service as a sort of acknowledgement, I supposed, that I have the physical apparatus to produce babies, even if I hadn't done the proper thing and done so. (I admit this is a jaundiced view and it may have been a terribly kind gesture acknowledging my parenting skills, but it made me feel like an object of pity.) Finally one year when my own lack of children just felt a bit too painful, I blew my stack and made my feelings known somewhat vociferously. Immediately my views were heard and it was realized that I was not alone but speaking for other childless women, married and single, and now we distribute our flowers differently! In an ideal church with an open and secure community these situations would not arise. Few churches are that idyllic however and the important point is that there should be such an atmosphere where those feelings can be expressed and heard. I am immensely grateful to the priest who was vicar at the time because he did not dismiss my feelings as those of a neurotic spinster, but instead listened to what I was saying, respected my views and changed things accordingly.

There are other issues around Mothering Sunday, though, and I am not the only childless person to find it difficult. The readings that are set, in the ASB at any rate, make it difficult to use the service creatively. They can of course be abandoned by an individual church – but a wider church which really wants to make single people feel included needs to give serious thought to the message it is conveying in lectionaries it compiles and in its use of language in general.

This leads on to the eternal problem of the family service. Most churches have one, on a once-a-month basis or more frequently, and its purpose varies from a free-for-all for young families to a real attempt at all-age worship, with all church members involved. But what is it to be called if it is not to appear to be catering for a particular group? Concerns about family services go much deeper than mere semantics of course, but I know of countless single people who simply do not go to the family service as they cannot cope with the jolly children and young parents aspect. It really should not be the business of a church to make any sub-group within its congregation feel excluded from a service. Some churches would perhaps do well to look at their services to see if a particular unwelcoming message is being conveyed.

Conversely, the family aspect of the church community is of immense importance for many people who live alone. It adds to the strength and vitality of any church when childless people have the opportunity to spend time with children. Many of the older single people – the grandparent age group – find those opportunities truly precious. One such person in my own church told me that she had not realized how much she had missed in not having children of her own until she was well over 70! Her love of children now is clear to see. It is obvious too that that feeling is entirely mutual. When a church community provides such a rich source of different relationships, all members benefit by it.

Being with children is important to many single people, particularly to those without younger members in their own families, but it does take a measure of trust before parents will feel easy about leaving their offspring with another adult. It is inevitable in today's climate that some will be suspicious of anyone who pays their children much attention at all and, sadly, churches are no more protected from claims of child abuse than any other community. Somehow a balance must be found between necessary caution and an atmosphere of trust. What is certainly true is that when parents can be sensitive to being part of the wider family of the church and generous in sharing their own family happiness with others, the benefits are enormous. Not only do they have a source of possible child-carers but their own friendships can be deepened, their interests extended, and the whole family enriched. Any church community which fails to use the rich mixture of people who enter its buildings has missed out on an important, God-given gift.

> When he gets to his pew and looks round him he sees just that selection of his neighbours whom he has hitherto avoided.[14]

Sometimes church communities are composed of just that group of people with whom we would rather *not* mix. It is then a difficult decision – are we to put up with it, recognize it as our problem rather than theirs, and make the most of an unpromising situation? Or rather will we then find ourselves floundering in a miserable mire, committed to a church which is not feeding us, thrown into the company of people with whom we have nothing in common? It is a problem for any Christian moving to a new area but for a single Christian whose emotional investment in a church could well be greater than that of a married one, it is something which requires careful consideration and prayer. Surely the best approach is not to over-commit yourself at an early stage. Rushing in and joining the choir, a home group, the coffee rota and signing up for the parish holiday may well feel like an ideal buffer against loneliness but might be entirely inappropriate. Joining anything to avoid facing up to being alone is almost always wrong: 'The person who comes into a fellowship because he is running away from himself is misusing it for the sake of diversion, no matter how spiritual this diversion may appear.'[15]

If a church is right for us, a place where we can truly feel part of the body of Christ, then many single people will feel an intense loyalty to that community – but what will help us to become involved more and to find personal affirmation?

Most people I have spoken to have mentioned their allegiance to a particular home group as being especially helpful. A well-established group like this deepens friendship and understanding, provides a number of people who will know us as individuals, and gives an opportunity to share at a deep level in the lives of others. My own home group is a place where we have shared sorrows and celebrations, where we have followed the enthusiasms and interests of particular members, where we have heard a vast variety of opinions from the orthodox to the heretical (certainly a place where I have received a tremendous amount of good advice, support in decision-making, a place to talk things over with people who will be on my side), but most of all it is somewhere where we have been able to laugh together. There is always the danger of any home group becoming a clique in which participants have run out of anything new to say to each other, but a number of long-term groups can be the bedrock of a Christian community.

> We do not read that Our Lord Himself ever played an instrument or enjoyed hearing others play theirs. The apostles did not attend concerts or go to dances .... Do you know what you're getting into? Is that any place for a Christian?[16]

Christians, whether deservedly or not, do not have the reputation of having a great deal of fun and there is something particularly depressing about the mere mention of a church social event. It immediately conjures up a picture of stultifying respectability, nice behaviour and everyone tucked up in their beds (their own beds, naturally – this is no place for lewdness) by 10.00 pm. Actually, most social gatherings need be nothing like that at all – and with luck even the respectability slips sometimes. But are they welcoming to single people? One friend, recently divorced, had the chilling experience of phoning for a ticket to a church supper and was asked in a tone of some surprise if she would not be coming with anyone. Needless to say, she made her excuses and did not go. The assumption that social events are for couples can be very deep-rooted.

It could perhaps be a positive policy for a church to ensure that social events are open to all and welcoming to those who will be attending without a partner. All the evidence, after all, seems to indicate that Jesus did not feel he had to take along a partner to the wedding at Cana or to the various fish suppers he dropped in on. Surely the emphasis should always be on including all the church family rather than making the comfortable feel even more comfortable.

Some events like theatre or concert visits will be easier for single people to attend than married couples – so if you are a single person at your own church, why not organize it yourself? You don't have to have a specific 'singles group' (horrid thought) in order to create a few social treats for fellow church members. Most people are only too pleased to find someone else who is willing to arrange tickets and there is nothing like stirring oneself out of natural indolence to cheer yourself up! Put up a notice or use the weekly bulletin – give it a try.

The best times to socialize with fellow church members, though, are the times that arise naturally – or perhaps in a contrived way that seems natural! I am thinking of having lunch together after taking a turn decorating the curate's house, dropping in for coffee after delivering leaflets – the sort of times when people feel familiar enough to be real friends because you have been working together.

Sadly, some churches can fail their single members badly. Some can remain unaware of truly painful loneliness, of desperate shyness that really needs a

great deal of warmth and welcoming to break it down
or of major crises looming in the lives of its members.
Others can jump in with a good deal too much enthusiasm and scare off those who really need to stay on
the sidelines and watch for a while. It is never easy to
get the balance right.

> Advice is seldom welcome and those who want it
> the most always like it the least.[17]

One of the little foibles that church people seem most
prone to is the passing on of helpful advice, little *bons
mots* designed to make your life that bit easier. Ha ha.
Among my favourites here is the well-known, 'When
you are married and have children of your own you
will know . . .', closely followed by, 'Of course children
make a house a home, don't they?' What am I supposed
to do, rent a few? One friend was congratulated in
much surprise by fellow Christians on having made a
real home for himself and as for his ability to cook,
well, he'll make a lovely husband one day, won't he?
(Actually he has, but that is neither here nor there.)

The Christmas period can bring out the worst in
advisers anxious to ensure that everyone shares in the
jollity, even those who have no nuclear family in their
immediate vicinity. One can feel positively bullied into
joining in the festivities and sometimes that is entirely
inappropriate. Single people have every right to keep
Christmas as they wish – oh and, by the way, we do
not 'go home for Christmas'; we go to stay with our
parents – our own homes are as valid as theirs.

It may sometimes seem ungrateful but it is quite
necessary to turn away invitations sometimes, to
refuse Sunday lunch because you have an important
engagement with yourself, to decline to be welcomed
into the bosom of another family. I have a personal
radar system which comes into operation if I think I

am being made into a good work – 'Must have Belinda round for a meal, she's all on her own, poor thing.' This is a signal for the poor thing to make herself scarce.

Hospitality is an important part of a loving community but so is the recognition of the need for privacy and a life of one's own. An overzealous community can take up so much of your time that it becomes impossible to make friends outside the church or to have time for yourself. Single people have more freedom to do as they wish – but that does not mean they should be willing to give it all away. Church communities are as vulnerable as any other to the bossy organizer whose mission in life is to get everyone else rushing about doing their bidding. It is essential to retain control over your own time and to get involved because you want to, not through an imposed parcel of guilt.

> Let him who cannot be alone beware of community. Let him who is not in community beware of being alone.[18]

Any single person brings particular gifts to a Christian community. Of course there is no guarantee that he or she will be a good listener but they will certainly have more opportunity to do so with a greater guarantee of confidentiality. Some marriages work on the premise that there are no secrets held from each other – which is hard luck if you have divulged to one partner a secret which you have no desire to have shared. Single people will have more time to commit to certain projects (with the proviso that no-one assumes they *must* commit it), perhaps to read more, to extend their own interests and to travel, all of which can stimulate a community. Broadening the mind and experience of one individual does affect other individuals. Just think of the times when you have heard someone speak with enthusiasm about one of their own interests: it is infectious.

It is often thought that a single Christian must do far more praying than the married ones, so I tried asking a few. One wailed, 'Belinda, I'm a *dreadful* pray-er!' Others looked furtive and guilty; still others said dubiously that they supposed that it must be true – all of which led me to believe that it is 'a practice more honoured in the breach than the observance'.[19] Martin Israel, in his book, *Living Alone* has some helpful advice for those who feel they could be using their prayer time as single people more profitably. He points out the opportunities there are for anyone who spends much time on their own to grow in spiritual awareness, the opportunity to listen to God rather than the chattering of a family. He sees the ministry of intercession for others who really do not have the time to pray themselves as an important function of the single Christian, and points out that 'By it more than in any other way, one ceases to be alone any longer but instead becomes the centre of an ever-enlarging circle of associates, friends and brothers.'[20]

Martin Israel mentions too what is probably the greatest gift which the single Christian can bring to our church communities (because I am not convinced that we are any better at praying than our married sisters and brothers!), and that is our presence. More than anything else in a church, people are impressed by those who turn up for things, who support church events, who will give them their undivided attention, chat about their lives, share amusing anecdotes and show an interest. If you have ever had a conversation with a parent who is constantly glancing around to see what horrors are being committed by a lively three year-old you will understand the value of someone who is simply interested in what you are saying. This is no reflection on the parents themselves; it is simply a product of parenthood. Nappies and naughtiness wait for no man.

Single people can be the core group of a church holiday or a parish retreat. They can be the organizers of charity events and social outings, stalwarts of the bazaar or the summer fête, the ones who will always be there to help with the washing up or the welcome group. Occasionally they can also be using the church as a power base – a focus for excess energy or a place in which inappropriate control is wielded. Some single people, not having a family of their own to boss about, can be tempted to use a church community for such a purpose. Before we get too involved in our own churches it is always salutary to question our own motives. Am I volunteering for this to get a handle on that? Am I putting all those hours in with an expectation of particular privileges? Am I enjoying the opportunity of participating in other people's lives a bit too much? This is Martin Israel again: 'Officious interference with the lives of other people in the guise of serving them is a common way of eluding the responsibilities in our own life, or deflecting our attention from our own inner deficiencies onto the troubles of another person.'[21]

If sometimes we discover that our motives are not as pure as we might wish, very often an awareness of that is all that is needed to change the situation. When we know what we are doing and can work out why we are doing it, we have far more control over our own actions. Praying that God might make us aware of our attempts to exercise power may not be a comfortable experience, but a bit of squirming undoubtedly does wonders for our immortal souls.

The community is the first place
where you will make God's kingdom incarnate.
It is one of the countless points
where God's new people assemble in peace . . .
Accept with gratitude
the brothers God gives you
to go with you on the way.
Your task is to serve and upbuild one another
as members of one body.[22]

When a church community is good it must be one
of the most supportive and stimulating influences
which any single person could have in their life. It is
a place where our abilities and strengths can be recog-
nized and valued, where individual differences are
something to glory in and where all the realities of
our lives can be brought to worship, an image of the
Kingdom of God in all its fullness. A place, in fact,
where we can feel completely ourselves and yet
completely a part of the body of Christ.

6

Looking to the future

Therefore do not worry about tomorrow,
for tomorrow will worry about itself.[1]

Worrying about the future is and always has been a
common enough pastime. We are encouraged to fret,
it seems, with every news report on the drugs problem
or crime or ecology or the Royal Family. What is going
to happen? Where is it all going to end? What can we
do to change the steady decline in standards in just
about everything? Once you have accepted that basically pessimistic view of the future there is nothing
to stop you from applying it to your own life and
becoming increasingly fearful. If you are single then
the temptation always is to think, 'If only I were not on
my own! I wouldn't need to worry about anything. I
would be financially secure. I would know where my
life was going.' It is all too easy to make the basic
assumption that there is something wrong with our
own lives and that it would really take another person
to make them right. A good antidote to that attitude is
to talk to a married person who is just as concerned
about their own future and worrying about what they
should be doing next. It suddenly becomes clear that
worries about the future are part of being human
rather than the private domain of the single person.

The solution to all our perceived problems cannot
depend on another person but must be found in our-

selves and in our relationship with God through prayer. It is not easy and the hardest part is waiting for the answers to our questions, the 'What am I supposed to do now?' questions. Please God, tell me as soon as possible. Experience shows time and time again that those questions do get answers, but somehow every time we hit one of those periods in our lives we are right back to square one, pleading with God for a quick-fix solution.

Nevertheless, as Christians we do have the huge advantage in life of knowing that we are not alone, that there is a Christian community to support us and that the Lord does provide, even if we are not instantly delighted with the provision.

The unexamined life is not worth living.[2]

The best place to start thinking about the future is in the present, looking at what we have in our lives and considering whether changes are really necessary. Sometimes we may be pleasantly surprised by that sort of review and discover that what we had been seeing as a bleak and loveless existence is actually full of rewards and a variety of valuable relationships. We may come to the conclusion that a major change is unnecessary and all that needs to be altered is our own attitude.

At other times we may decide that it would be good to move house or consider a job change or a major career move. It is at times like that when a single person can feel most isolated – when decisions have to be made alone. One friend speaks of the time when he had to make a judgement about a job which had been offered to him, a very different path from the one which he had mapped out for himself, as one of the loneliest times of his life. It is not easy taking momentous decisions when you realize that you are the only one who can do it, and that no-one else really has any right to a say in the matter, no matter how good their advice. At such times one longs for someone to share in the process, not as adviser but as a co-decision-maker. I cannot do this on my own! Surely someone else can have a say?

The feeling of isolation will lessen if we do not feel pressurized to make a major decision within a limited time span, so that we can listen to all the advice, have time to pray about it and come to a calm and rational conclusion. There will be occasions when time is an unavailable luxury though, and then we find ourselves praying frantically and hoping for the best.

It is essential then that we do not lead unexamined lives but have taken time to think through what we want from life. The general slushy feeling that 'I just want to be happy' is actually not particularly realistic, and drifting along looking vaguely for happiness is not likely to work particularly effectively. Happiness does not last for ever and it cannot be held on to, so as an ambition the pursuit of happiness is not likely to pay dividends. To set goals and consider ambitions is vital if we are not to look back on a lifetime of wasted opportunities in later life. I am not suggesting that we should all be rushing around with a personal timetable for promotion in a professional life of startling success. The goals can be as simple as to have a holiday abroad this year, or to make time for a particular interest, or to set time aside for community or church work. The end result should be a sense of achievement and a feeling that we have something to show for it. If you are single you have to show yourself, without getting neurotic about it, that life is good and you are making it good.

The alternative route is to be the passive pawn of circumstances and that will leave us feeling powerless and without any say in our lives. It is usually the case that we can control events far more than at first appears possible, and when we do take control we switch from a feeling of helplessness to one of growing confidence and self-reliance. I recently had my car stolen, which left me first of all quite shocked and then feeling I was unable to control what was happening. It was not until I had arranged a lift into school the next day, phoned the insurers, and seen the police that I regained some sense of my own strength. Before that, it felt as if the car thieves had robbed me of far more than a vehicle – my independence, my sense of personal security and my whole way of life felt threatened.

I have to confess too that I even caught myself thinking 'Now if I were married, I wouldn't have to go through this alone . . .', but it was a married friend who spoke of a similar feeling of isolation brought on by any crisis. In most crises we are alone, married or single, and 'going through things together' does not always serve to strengthen relationships. My own sneaking feeling that really I needed a husband to get me through it was no more than the old familiar, 'if only certain things were different, I would have a wonderful life' syndrome in yet another disguise. We do *not* need another person to get us through and things are not different; they are as they are. Most of us will find the resources within ourselves to deal with most crises – and those of us who are Christians know that it is at times of crisis that we can be most aware of God's powerful presence alongside us.

> One might argue that people who have no abiding interests other than their spouses and families are as limited intellectually as those who have neither spouse nor children may be emotionally.[3]

Interests and enthusiasms are, or can be, an important

part of anyone's life, and the time and opportunity to follow those interests will be increased for those whose lives are more solitary than others. Even when the interests are the sort which draw us into contact with all sorts of different people and enable us to live a rich and varied existence, there can be a tendency to think of them as 'child substitutes' or as compensation for a broken heart. There is no reason why we should accept that analysis of our own interests or why we should feel that an enthusiasm for painting or calligraphy or medieval history should be a less valid way of spending our time than investing it in a family.

Anthony Storr's book on solitude was originally published under the title *The School of Genius*. In it he argues that women and men of genius have had much more room to explore their particular studies by reason of their solitary lives than if they had been married with a family. Modesty forbids that I should speak of myself in quite the same breath as Edward Gibbon or any of the other geniuses about whom Storr writes (well, modesty and the hoots of derision of my acquaintances when I utter such statements), but I do value the time I can spend on my interests; as Storr says, interests can 'play a greater part in the economy of human happiness than modern psycho-analysts and their followers allow'. Indeed, he goes on to say that, 'it is only since Freud advanced the notion that heterosexual fulfilment is the *sine qua non* of mental health that anyone would question Gibbon's status as a more than commonly happy and successful human being.' The cynicism of the present age dictates that we should look for a sexual motive in the actions of most people, particularly those in the public eye. While there is no doubt that sex is a powerful impulse, so are other aspects of our psyche. Our interests do not have to be a compensation for anything, let alone for sex.

They can be time-consuming passions without any sexual motive at all and can certainly be life-enhancing.

It is sad sometimes when single people bury themselves in their work or an interest simply in order to avoid facing up to their lives but this is not how it has to be. Writing *The Decline and Fall of the Roman Empire* is almost certainly as good a *raison d'être* as any other and, who knows?, the sense of fulfilment and achievement might have been as great for Gibbon as fatherhood would be for another man.

The single person does need to beware the tendency to let work take over their life and to realize that he or she can be susceptible to becoming a workaholic. One retired friend said that in looking over her working life, she realized that she had overdone the work part and let it expand to fill a vacuum. She spoke of the need to discipline oneself not to spend longer on a task than others might, not to give in to that impulse to stay on just a bit longer to get something done. It is important to take a pride in your work but it is equally important to leave time for yourself. On reaching retirement it will be the interests in your life that can go on and they can take as much or as little of your time as you wish. People who have spent every second of their waking hours involved in their paid employment may well find themselves completely without aim or purpose when that employment ceases. Single people will inevitably be more prone to that temptation than their married counterparts who will have another person to help redress the balance, so it is essential to have thought of it before it is too late.

Interests have to be planned for and you have to find the time and energy for them. And to do that, you have to first dismiss the feeling of guilt about spending time on something that is essentially for yourself. Even finding time to read a book can sometimes make a person feel guilty, if they have been brought up to feel they must always keep busy in practical ways. If you have had it drummed into you from an early age that you must be at work in order to be using your time properly, it is going to be hard to relax on your own without a partner telling you to stop. But stopping and learning to relax is essential to relieve current stress as well as to build future hobbies.

> Grow old along with me!
> The best is yet to be,
> The last of life, for which the first was made!
> Our times are in His hand
> Who said, 'A whole I planned,
> Youth shows but half; trust God: see all, nor
> be afraid!'[4]

I have yet to find anyone who looks forward to increasing age with eager anticipation. There are fears of ill-health, of a gradual decline in one's faculties and of possible loneliness and isolation. It is said that friends are much harder to make when one is older, when we have all become set in our ways. For the single person there are additional fears, of being a lonely old man or woman, with no children of one's own to take an interest, no grandchildren to show for all those years of existence, no life to look back on with fond memories, no partner in one's old age.

So much for the fears – what about the reality? First of all there is no hard and fast rule that all older people have to become set in their ways. We have all known lively, broad-minded 70 year-olds and dull, conservative 30 year-olds. What makes the difference is not age but attitude. For anyone who is involved in a church community with a wide age range there is every opportunity to keep a youthful attitude of mind – we are not limited to our own contemporaries when making friendships. Often younger people will welcome the chance to make older friends with a breadth of experience. Older does not have to equal boring any more than single has to equal unfulfilled. Older friends I have spoken to do cite some advantages as well as the disadvantages of increasing years. One is that regrets lessen, as the acceptance of one's lifestyle and marital status arrives. Tolerance can increase after a lifetime of working with a range of different people and with the benefit of hindsight it is often possible to see that things have worked out for the best, even the things that felt intolerable at the time.

It is interesting that many of the older age range of single people still do not think of themselves as dyed-in-the-wool spinsters or bachelors and still speak in terms of 'well, I suppose I'm not likely to meet someone now, but . . .'. One of the things that came as a bit of a revelation to me, when I began to make a concerted effort to find out what it was like to be older and single, was that most people I spoke to were incurable romantics. Responses ranged from those who said 'If I can't have the one I wanted, why settle for second-best?' to 'If there had been someone to sweep me off my feet then of course I would have gone.' Could it be that part of the decision to remain single stems originally from a highly romanticized view of one's ideal mate? If it is so, no-one to whom I have spoken has regretted it for an instant! There is still the lingering thought, even if it is not expressed as a hope, that perhaps one day . . . . Dreams never disappear, whatever the age and as the Preacher says in Ecclesiastes, 'Anyone who is among the living has hope – even a live dog is better off than a dead lion!'[5]

All I'm asking, Tusker, is did you mean it when you

said I'd been a good woman to you? And if so, why
did you leave me? Why did you leave me here? I am
frightened to be alone, Tusker, although I know it is
wrong and weak to be frightened –
– but now, until the end, I shall be alone.[6]

I had always vaguely suspected that growing older
is much more difficult for the single than the married,
but in some ways the fears and worries seem to be
more intensified when you are feeling them on behalf
of someone else. There is the fear of being the one left
to carry on alone, as the widow I have quoted above
finds at the end of Paul Scott's novel *Staying On*. Even
though her marriage was far from easy it was the only
life she had known – and what was left when that had
gone? There is the possibility of one's partner suffering
a stroke or being the victim of a debilitating illness, so
that one suddenly becomes responsible for some difficult and patience-stretching nursing, becoming one of
the hard-pressed carers of our society. There can
sometimes be the problem of having to go through an
extended period of retirement with someone who has
become downright cantankerous and irritable, no
longer the alluring idol of one's dreams and in fact a
bit of a trial to live with. There is often the worry of
becoming a burden on someone else; 'For richer, for
poorer, in sickness and in health'[7] can be an awesome
responsibility and not one we wish to land on our
loved ones.

For many married people in their 70s or 80s the
prospect of having to learn to live alone when they
have never done so is extremely alarming. Those of us
who are single have built up all sorts of defences, support systems and survival mechanisms, most of which
we are not even aware of. Some we cannot pass on as
good advice because we do not know that we do it.

Cooking for one, when you have been used to cooking for a family, is often too much bother, while for anyone who is single it is just common sense. The whole business of looking after yourself is second nature to the single person but a massive hurdle to some who are suddenly left alone.

Increasing age and infirmity is not a welcome prospect for anyone, but for the single, perhaps, it is something we have already acted out in our illnesses suffered alone, the crises we have struggled to cope with, and the loneliness we have learned to overcome.

I always imagine that clergymen need wives to help them with their parish work but I suppose most of his congregation are devout elderly women with nothing much to do, so that's all right.[8]

Many churches seem to have a few devout elderly ladies as their most stalwart members. The church has obviously become the mainstay of their lives, whether single or widowed, and in many ways they have become the mainstay of their church. They may have the time for intercessory prayer or the time to devote to others which is often denied to a younger group of people. I remember pointing out just such a faithful elderly lady to a friend. She attended her church daily, a devoted and devout person whose life had now shrunk to encompass very little else. I wondered aloud whether I would one day become such a person, and I must admit that it was with a slight feeling of trepidation. 'Of course you will,' he said, 'you're well on the way already.' At the time I felt inclined to hit him but now I suspect that it is actually rather a pleasant prospect. Serving God in his church and in the world must be the aim of any Christian and if in later years we can look forward to the rhythm and routine of prayer as a structure to our day we have certainly got something to look forward to.

But before reaching that stage, many of us will have the energy in retirement to devote to more practical ways of service and, like our interests, those need to be planned for. Single people approaching retirement need to consider how they are going to fill their time. Retirement itself can be a major loss which has to be worked through. If you have enjoyed your job and really thrown yourself into it, then you will inevitably miss it. Many retired teachers will deeply regret not seeing children on a regular basis; business people might miss the travel and excitement of their working lives, and others will find the sudden loss of all apparent status a real blow. It is often the case for single people that they have invested a great deal of emotion in their paid employment and you cannot cut off that sort of investment without feeling a hurt.

One of the biggest shocks, retired single friends tell me, is that of suddenly discovering there is no-one to talk to. There are some things that really need to be spoken aloud, if only to get them off our chests. Events in the news which have shocked or touched us, people we have encountered who have irritated or inspired us, the weather changes (we are British, after all) – all these things we have been used to discussing with our colleagues. Suddenly there is no-one whom we will see and sound off to, and most visitors can be a little overwhelmed if they are greeted with a list of grievances and/or news items as they cross the threshold. There is an adjustment that has to be made and most people seem to find it takes at least a year to settle into it.

The temptation will be to fill the day so that there is no time to sit and brood, but that should almost certainly be resisted. Most retired people seem to have experienced the feeling that they cannot imagine how they found the time to work. There will be a great variety of ways in which we can use our time, perhaps connected with previous employment or community or charity work as well as involvement in the church (and goodness knows that can expand to fill any vacuum), but the best advice is probably to be cautious about accepting time-filling jobs. You can always increase the time you spend on most of those pursuits, but cutting back is rather more difficult.

Most people seem to feel a need for a routine in their lives in order to contribute to a sense of well-being. A daily routine is conducive to a natural rhythm of health and anyone living alone is going to have to impose that for themselves. A certain amount of self-discipline will be needed and it will be easier to establish if there are a few fixed events during the week. Clubs which meet regularly or charity shops which need a consistent pattern of help might sound stultifyingly monotonous to some, but others will find them a lifeline.

Many single people will find the duty to care for aged parents thrust upon them, just when they were hoping for some free time for themselves. Such duties can be onerous and wearing, but many will feel that it is something they must do for the people who gave them so much. What can and should be escaped is a feeling that any newly retired single person can now be the dogsbody of anyone who cares to demand their time. No-one deserves to start their retirement by being duped out of all their free time by a manipulative relative or friend, however infirm, and long, hard consideration must be given before any commitment is made. Guilt is a powerful weapon in the hands of a ruthless person, who may well play on the Christian calling to compassion to their own ends. As one older friends says, 'Do it for love, or not at all.'

Man is the only creature who can see his own death coming; and when he does, it concentrates his mind wonderfully. He prepares for death by freeing himself from mundane goals and attachments and turns instead to the cultivation of his own interior garden.[9]

Getting older inevitably involves intimations of mortality – gradual energy loss, debilitating diseases, and the deaths of contemporaries all underline the startling fact that I will not live for ever, even if I do feel just the same as I did at 18 or 36. Police officers look scarcely old enough to be in high school and the world is suddenly full of young whippersnappers who are a darn sight too bumptious for their own good. It may well be even more difficult for single people to accept their increasing years, without grandchildren to show them that they are ageing. But every age has its advantages as well as its disadvantages and old age and even contemplating one's own end does not have to be as mournful an occupation as it sounds.

There can be a feeling of freedom from a certain pattern of behaviour – after all, if you cannot take liberties in your later years, when can you? There can be a blessed release in looking back at your life and realizing that you do not have to do all those things that people expected you to do before. There can be a feeling that instead of being a doer you can at last be a receiver.

The feeling that the world is arranged in couples dissipates too, because more and more people find themselves on their own again. One older single friend tells me that she is not always as sympathetic with widows as she should be, but I do not suppose she shows it! There can be greater opportunities to be an individual or even to become mildly eccentric. Age can be a licence to do as you wish. There are pitfalls, naturally; it is not desirable to become so downright odd that all your acquaintances begin to adopt subtle avoidance procedures, but old age can be a time of non-conformity, a great relief for those who had found conforming a bit of a strain. Many single people have not married for that very reason, so they will be well placed to enjoy the freedom of age.

There will be some fears that are the same for all, whatever their marital status. The fear of becoming too infirm to look after oneself looms large for some, and then the possibility of taking out an insurance policy for long-term care might be explored. One person I spoke to was even considering putting her name down for a home as a provision for extreme old age, although she did not seem wildly enthusiastic about it!

The fear of losing independence and control is a very real one, although many people continue to exert control by planning and paying for their funerals. A very independent single lady from my own church had done exactly that, so that when her funeral recently came there was no doubt about her wishes for readings, readers or music, and she had even stipulated that she wanted to go to the crematorium alone – a fierce defender of her right to 'go it alone' to the very end.

If you live alone and particularly if you have had one or two scares about your health, the worry of possibly collapsing and not being able to get help can be a very real one. One person spoke of it as a 'burden of fear', the 'if something happens, what do I do?' thought. The stress of that sort of fear can actually contribute to ill health, so that setting up emergency procedures with friends and neighbours can be beneficial, whether it is a visible sign in the window or an emergency telephone number. It can help too to make sure that there is someone locally who will be named 'next of kin' in an emergency – the person to be contacted does not have to be a blood relative. Another suggestion from an older friend is to put a red star in your address book beside all those whom you would wish to be informed of a serious illness. By doing that sort of thing you have established some sort of control, a great antidote to stress and fear.

> 'Ronald,' said Elizabeth, 'your clothes are really pretty and your hair is very neat. You look like a real prince but you are a bum.'
> They didn't get married after all.[10]

The number of people who actually plan to live a single life must be quite small; most of us, like Elizabeth the paper bag princess, just find ourselves that way. I have tried to show in this book that it is not at all a bad place to find yourself and that you may well do exactly that: find yourself, the real you. If, however, you are thinking 'this is all very well, but being single is just not me; I know I must find another way', then it is time to look at the alternatives. They are all going to require some effort, which is probably why a sort of innate laziness urges me to do otherwise! It is useful to sit down and write a list of all alternative courses, however bizarre. Try to be realistic. Tom Cruise and Pamela Anderson are already spoken for, so dropping them a line to mention that you are available could lead to disappointment. But the list might include such suggestions as dating agencies, joining a singles group, joining a Christian community short-term, or taking a year or more out to travel or to work for a charity or aid agency abroad, exploring a vocation.

Then go through the list and think of your reaction to each suggestion. If your real, truthful response to all of those proposals is 'forget it!', then do, and look at your single life again. Maybe it is not so bad after all. In looking at the list, beware of blinding yourself to your real motivation, because lying to yourself is generally a mistake. So do not kid yourself that your impulse to apply for a mission partner position is noble and self-sacrificing if actually you are trying to use the situation as a sort of Christian Foreign Legion. You will be found out. Charities and missionary societies need people with a vocation not a neurosis. If you do meet a possible marriage partner then never, ever, think 'this is my last chance and I have to take it'. Many unhappy marriages are founded on such a decision and even if you have got to screaming point about being single, bear in mind that the screaming would be much worse if you were unhappily trapped. Most of us have felt pretty desperate at some time or another – friends' weddings, Valentine's Day, Leap Year's Day – but we have survived it. (I know it sounds silly, but the tradition of women being able to do the proposing on 29 February can lead to great regret that there is no-one worth proposing to, while some branches of the Samaritans find that 14 February is their busiest day.) What God has provided for us here and now should be sufficient. It may not feel like it but it should be, so look at it and see.

In *The Remains of the Day*[11] Mr Stevens the butler is the archetypal deeply unhappy single man, a man who has repressed all his emotions and thrown aside his only chance of love. At the end of the story he is made aware that the whole premise of his life, that his work in service must always come first and his own needs a very poor second, has been a mistake. He tries to make amends but it is too late. There are some who seem to think that every single person must be nursing a similarly broken heart, with all their emotions banked down and a burden of bitterness which they

113

will carry all their days. But bitterness is not confined to single people and certainly need not be part of a Christian's life. It is not an easy task to disperse such sadness, and sometimes anger and hatred can burst through when we are under the impression that we have dealt with them thoroughly, but they will dissipate with persistent prayer. It is not clear at the end of the novel if Mr Stevens will ever break free of his sadness and his feeling that his mistakes can never be rectified: 'I trusted I was doing something worthwhile. I can't even say I made my own mistakes. Really – one has to ask oneself – what dignity is there in that?'

We all have the opportunity to make our own mistakes, to take charge of our own lives and to preserve our own dignity and it is the hope of all Christians that the God who makes all things new can help us through such traumas to find peace on the other side.

> Those who hope in the Lord will renew their strength. They will soar on wings like eagles; they will run and not grow weary, they will walk and not be faint.[12]

The single life, a life alone, has its dangers and its pitfalls but I have tried to show that it is, or can be, a good life and a life full of rewards. Repining and casting envious eyes on others is really not much fun, and in the end the Christian life must be about living life to the full.

There are many aspects to being single which make it a gift, if we decide to treat it as such. It does depend very much on our own attitude and the way we see ourselves: if we value our way of life it will be perceived as a good one; if we devalue it then no-one else will think much of it either.

I shall let one of the wonderful Barbara Pym's absurd clergymen have the last word:

'It is really much wiser for a man to stay single', said the Archdeacon, 'and then it doesn't matter if he's late for lunch.'[13]

Notes

All Bible quotations are from the *New International Version*, copyright © 1973, 1978, 1984 by the International Bible Society. Published by Hodder & Stoughton.

Introduction

1 John 10.10.
2 1 Thessalonians 5.18.
3 Artemus Ward (Charles Farrar Browne), 1834–67.

1 True to myself

1 Galatians 6.4–5.
2 Shakespeare, *Henry V*, II, iii.
3 Teach us, good Lord, to serve Thee as Thou deservest,
   To give and not to count the cost:
   To fight and not to heed the wounds:
   To toil and not to seek for rest:
   To labour and not to ask for any reward
   Save that of knowing that we do thy will.
   St Ignatius Loyola, 'Prayer for Generosity' in *Oxford Book of Prayer* (Oxford University Press 1985).
4 Quoted by Wendy Robinson in *Exploring Silence* (Fairacres 1974).
5 Luke 14.18.
6 Isaiah 6.8.
7 Psalm 142.3.
8 Kenneth Grahame, *The Wind in the Willows* (Methuen & Co. Ltd 1908).
9 Richard Lovelace (1618–58), 'To Althea, from prison'.
10 *The Cloud of Unknowing* (Penguin Books Ltd 1961).

11 Kenneth Grahame, *The Wind in the Willows*.
12 Babette Cole, *Princess Smartypants* (Hamish Hamilton Ltd 1986).

2 Being alone

1   Luke 5.16.
2   Deuteronomy 30.19.
3   George and Weedon Grossmith, *The Diary of a Nobody*, first appeared in *Punch* and was published in book form in 1892 by permission of the publishers Messrs Bradbury & Agnew.
4   Parson James Woodforde, *The Diary of a Country Parson, 1758–1802* (Oxford University Press 1935).
5   Genesis 2.18.
6   Delia Smith, *One is Fun* (Hodder & Stoughton 1985).
7   Jill Murphy, *Five Minutes Peace* (Walker Books Ltd 1986).
8   Anthony de Mello, *Awareness* (Fount Paperbacks © 1990 by the Center for Spiritual Exchange).
9   Isaac Bickerstaffe 1735–1812.
10 Anthony de Mello, *Awareness*.
11 Alan Bennett, *Talking Heads* (BBC Books 1988).
12 Samuel Taylor Coleridge (1772–1834), 'The Ancient Mariner'.
13 Dietrich Bonhoeffer, *Life Together* (first published under the title of *Gemeinsames Leben* by Chr Kaiser Verlag, Munich; first British edition SCM Press 1954).
14 *The Observer*, 11 February 1996.
15 Charles Dickens, *Great Expectations* (1860–1) (Penguin Books).
16 Samuel Taylor Coleridge, 'The Ancient Mariner'.

3 Friends and relatives

1   Proverbs 17.17.
2   1 Corinthians 13.
3   John 13.34.
4   John 15.13–14.
5   C. S. Lewis, *The Four Loves* (Geoffrey Bles 1960).

6   1 Corinthians 13.7.

7   P. G. Wodehouse, *Very Good, Jeeves* (Herbert Jenkins Ltd 1930).

8   Ruth 1.16.

9   Ruth 2.11–12.

10 1 Timothy 5.8.

11 Matthew 12.48.

12 Michael Palin and Terry Jones, *Ripping Yarns* (Eyre Methuen Ltd 1978).

13 *Issues in Human Sexuality*. A Statement by the House of Bishops (Church House Publishing 1991).

14 M. Scott Peck, *The Road Less Travelled* (Hutchinson & Co 1983).

15 C. S. Lewis, *The Four Loves*.

16 *Issues in Human Sexuality*.

17 1 Samuel 20.42.

18 2 Samuel 1.26.

19 From the hymn 'In Christ there is no east or west', John Oxenham (1852–1941).

20 John Donne (1571–1631), *Devotions upon Emergent Occasions* (1624) (The Nonesuch Press).

4 Love and sexuality

1   1 Corinthians 13.2.

2   M. Scott Peck, *The Road Less Travelled*.

3   Matthew 25.28–9.

4   *Kilvert's Diary*, 1870–9, Swindon, 20 November 1870 (Penguin; one-volume selection first published by Jonathan Cape 1944).

5   Jane Austen, *Pride and Prejudice*, 1813.

6   2 Corinthians 5.17.

7   P. G. Wodehouse, *Nothing Serious* (Herbert Jenkins Ltd 1950).

8   P. G. Wodehouse, *Very Good, Jeeves*.

9   Anthony de Mello, *Awareness*.

10 *Sunday Telegraph* 27 August 1995.

11 Shakespeare, *Hamlet*, III, i.

12 1 Corinthians 7.7.

13 1 Corinthians 7.9.

14 Matthew 19.11–13.

15 1 Corinthians 7.34.

16 1 Thessalonians 4.4.

17 Anthony de Mello, *Awareness*.

18 1 Thessalonians 5.18.

19 Matthew 12.48.

20 From the third Eucharistic Prayer, from *The Order for Holy Communion Rite A, The Alternative Service Book 1980*.

5 The Church community

1   1 Corinthians 12.27.

2   *Something to Celebrate*, Report of a Working Party of the Board for Social Responsibility (Church House Publishing 1995).

3   *Something to Celebrate*.

4   1 Corinthians 7.8.

5   Matthew 22.37.

6   *Something to Celebrate*.

7   Anthony Storr, *Solitude* (Flamingo 1989; first published under the title *The School of Genius*, André Deutsch 1988).

8   Dietrich Bonhoeffer, *Life Together*.

9   James Thurber, *Vintage Thurber* Vol. 1 (Penguin Books 1983, first published Hamish Hamilton 1963).

10 George Orwell, *A Clergyman's Daughter* (first published Gollancz 1935, Penguin Books 1964).

11 Barbara Pym, *Some Tame Gazelle* (Jonathan Cape 1950).

12 Barbara Pym, *Excellent Women* (Jonathan Cape 1952).

13 *Issues in Human Sexuality*.

14 C. S. Lewis, *The Screwtape Letters* (Geoffrey Bles: The Centenary Press 1942).

15 Dietrich Bonhoeffer, *Life Together*.

16 Garrison Keillor, *We are Still Married* (Faber & Faber 1989).

17 Philip Dormer Stanhope, 4th Earl of Chesterfield (1694–1773), 29 January 1748.

18 Dietrich Bonhoeffer, *Life Together*.
19 Shakespeare, *Hamlet*, I, iv.
20 Martin Israel, *Living Alone* (SPCK 1982).
21 Martin Israel, *Living Alone*.
22 *Rule for a New Brother* by the Brakkenstein Community of the Blessed Sacrament Fathers, Holland (Darton Longman and Todd 1973).

6 Looking to the future

1   Matthew 6.34.
2   Socrates, 469–399 BC. (Plato, The Last Days of Socrates (Penguin Classics).
3   Anthony Storr, *Solitude*.
4   Robert Browning (1812–89), *Rabbi ben Ezra* (1864).
5   Ecclesiastes 9.4.
6   Paul Scott, *Staying On* (William Heinemann Ltd 1977).
7   The Marriage Service, *The Alternative Service Book 1980*.
8   Barbara Pym, *Excellent Women*.
9   Anthony Storr, *Solitude*.
10 Robert N. Munsch, *The Paper Bag Princess* (Annick Press Ltd, Toronto, Canada 1980).
11 Kazuo Ishiguro, *The Remains of the Day* (Faber & Faber Ltd 1989).
12 Isaiah 40.31.
13 Barbara Pym, *Some Tame Gazelle*.